Relationship Marketing and Customer Relationship Management

Editors

Annekie Brink

Adele Berndt

JUTA

Relationship Marketing and Customer Relationship Management
First published 2008

ISBN 978-0-70217-739-2

Project Manager: Sharon Steyn
Editor: Alex Potter
Proofreader: Fiona Potter
Typesetter: Unwembi Communications
Indexer: Cecily Van Gend
Cover Designer: Marius Roux
Printed: Pinetown Printers

Preface

As marketing entered the 1990s, the relationship marketing concept represented a new marketing paradigm, a shift in business thinking, and was regarded as the biggest change in 50 years, in effect taking marketing back to its roots. The relationship marketing philosophy, through its implementation in customer relationship management (CRM), became the 'battle cry' of the 1990s.

Marketers are aware of the importance of customers and customer retention for the long-term survival of their organisations. This is reflected in the shift that has taken place within marketing – from transactional marketing to building long-term relationships with customers.

Relationships are the fundamental asset of an organisation. More than anything else, relationships determine the future of the organisation. Relationships predict whether new value will continue to be created and shared with the customer. If customers are amenable to a deepening bond, they will do more business with the organisation. If employees like to work there, they will continue along their learning curve and produce more and better. If investors and bankers are happy with their returns, they will continue to keep their funds in the organisation. The purpose of CRM is thus to create meaningful relationships with strategically significant parties and indicate how these relationships can be created on a one-to-one basis.

In terms of CRM, all customers are not equal; thus different customers need to be treated differently. CRM recognises the key role that individual customers play; thus the most profitable customers have to be identified, so that an organisation can focus on customers appropriate to its strategy.

CRM is technology driven. By using technology appropriately, an organisation can serve customers as individuals. However, technology is merely the facilitator of CRM and does not solve any problems a business may have. Before any organisation decides to deploy CRM technology, it must first include customer centricity as part of its corporate vision and mission.

Today, many organisations realise the importance of CRM, but most still operate with a mixture of the transactional and the relational marketing approaches. By building relationships, organisations are able to obtain competitive advantage in the marketplace over their competitors, thus increasing their overall profitability and success.

Implementing a CRM strategy in an organisation can require extensive changes in the way in which the organisation does business. A CRM strategy requires changing the processes, training and leadership of the organisation. It thus requires a total transformation!

In this text we focus on the basic principles of the relationship marketing philosophy and what is required in an organisation to implement CRM successfully. One important element necessary for the implementation of CRM is excellent customer service, so this is dealt with in detail. We also focus on the individual customer approach, business-to-business markets and how to build relationships with all key stakeholders. In the last two chapters we show how a CRM strategy could be planned and implemented.

Contributors

Prof A Brink – Unisa (Chapters 1, 2, and 8)
Prof M Cant – Unisa (Chapter 3)
Prof A Berndt – University of Johannesburg (Chapter 4, 5, 6, 7 and 9)

Plan of this book

This book focuses on the following components of Relationship Marketing (RM) and Customer Relationship Management (CRM):

Chapter 1	The nature of Relationship Marketing (RM) and Customer Relationship Management (CRM)	In this chapter, the philosophies of RM and CRM are introduced, as well as the organisational requirements of these philosophies.
Chapter 2	Building customer relationships	This chapter focuses on the nature of relationships, the driving forces of relationships, customer retention through customer bonding and the lifetime value of customers.
Chapter 3	Service issues in RM and CRM	This chapter deals with the various dimensions of service and their effect on relationship building issues.
Chapter 4	Internal marketing	Employees interact with the customer on a daily basis, and these are the people who can have the greatest effect on customer behaviour. Employees form a crucial group with whom the organisation needs to develop relationships, as is examined in this chapter.
Chapter 5	One-to-one marketing and Mass customisation	For needs to be met, customers are able to have products specifically developed to satisfy their needs, a process known as customisation. How organisations can customise their products and services is discussed in this chapter.
Chapter 6	Business to business relationships	Relationships that are built with customers differ from those that are developed and maintained with other business organisations, such as suppliers and competitors. These relationships form the focus of this chapter.
Chapter 7	Stakeholders in relationship marketing	This chapter examines the way in which organisations build relationships with other stakeholders, such as the community and the intermediaries in the distribution channel.
Chapter 8	Planning a CRM strategy	This chapter details the suggested stages in the CRM planning process. A business must actually plan how it will create, implement and manage a programme to ensure building relationships with its customers
Chapter 9	Implementing CRM in an organisation	All plans have to be implemented if they are to be regarded as a success. Implementing CRM faces a number of challenges and these are discussed in this final chapter.

Content

CHAPTER

1

The Nature of Relationship Marketing (RM) and Customer Relationship Management (CRM)

Learning Outcomes

After studying this chapter, you should be able to:

- explain how relationship marketing (RM) and customer relationship management (CRM) evolved from the marketing concept

- compare the traditional marketing approach and the relationship marketing approach

- illustrate the focus areas of RM

- explain the new capabilities that an organisation requires to implement RM and CRM.

1.1   Introduction

During the 1980s, marketers began to realise that marketing, once the leading department in an organisation, was losing its primacy to other organisational disciplines and doing little to resolve the problem. The marketing function was being marginalised, with many well-known companies, such as Proctor & Gamble and Unilever, abolishing the position of marketing director to concentrate on other functional activities.[1]

Many companies were beginning to question the large expenditure on marketing without a measurable return on investment that had been assumed in past decades. Most brands showed very little growth, and markets became dominated by oligopolies. Branding, originally conceived to provide customers with quality assurance, had, over time, evolved into a segmentation tool, with different brands for each segment. It also became obvious that strategic competitive advantage could no longer be delivered on the basis of product and service characteristics alone, since there was little difference between products. Because of this, customers were bombarded with advertising messages to increase organisations' profitability.

Marketing was being openly criticised for lack of innovation in the face of hostile markets, and for largely adopting defensive strategies to cope with this situation. Marketers of the period generally made the mistake of seeing marketing as a functional discipline rather than as an integrated business process.[2] Marketing managers were practising marketing management, but not marketing-oriented management.[3] Moreover, marketers were so busy attending to the practice of marketing that they may not have noticed that it was in crisis. It became clear that the marketing mix and other aspects of traditional marketing were dying.[4] Some authors went so far as to suggest that 'Marketing is dead because the old rules of identifying and satisfying customer demand no longer apply. Technology has seen to that and, in the process, created entirely new opportunities for marketers.'[5] The world was changing, but marketing appeared to be stuck in a rut.

As marketing entered the 1990s, relationship marketing — a new marketing paradigm and a shift in business thinking — was regarded as the biggest change in 50 years, in effect taking marketing back to its roots. The relationship marketing concept evolved from the marketing concept. It is therefore necessary to look first at the marketing concept.

1.2   The Marketing Concept

The marketing concept was conceptualised in the 1950s by marketing scholars such as Peter Drucker:[6] 'Marketing ... is the whole business seen from the point of view of its final result, that is, from the customer's point of view.'

The essence of the marketing concept is in understanding customer needs and wants, thus the focus is on the customer. If a company offers goods and services that satisfy the needs of and create value for the customer — providing customer satisfaction and the right customer-perceived quality — the company stands the best chance of maximising profitability.

This customer focus has become a widespread slogan, but it is understood and implemented only by a few of those who express it. Although rational in principle, it was flawed in practice. The actual needs, wants and expectations of the customer were, in fact, not perceived in reality as of paramount importance. Thus, while lip service was paid to customer supremacy in principle, in practice, marketers ignored it.[7]

One can therefore say that the marketing concept has failed in its implementation over the last 20 years or more. However, it is not only the marketing concept that is flawed, but the whole traditional marketing approach, and in particular, aspects such as the 4 Ps of marketing (product, price, promotion, place), transactional marketing and market segmentation.

1.3   The Traditional Marketing Approach

As we have seen, it became evident that 'customer supremacy' — the central tenet of the marketing concept and marketing — although rational in principle, was flawed in practice. Despite the claims to the contrary, the actual needs, wants and expectations of the customer were not perceived in reality as being of paramount importance.[8]

We will first look at the traditional marketing mix, followed by transactional marketing and market segmentation.

1.3.1 The Marketing Mix

The marketing mix, as marketers have traditionally considered it, comprised a combination of marketing variables, with emphasis on those components they deemed important in securing, satisfying and retaining customers.[9] This marketing mix bundled product (including the service), price, promotion and distribution options together according to the marketer's predetermined assessment of the value to each segment, and the most efficient and effective means of providing value. With this approach, planning and execution were orderly. In terms of the marketing mix, the company made all the key decisions regarding the research that would be conducted, the product concept and the value that would be provided, the advertising message, and the services that would be delivered to a segment. Customers within each segment were served as though they all wanted the same thing. Remember Henry Ford's reply, 'You can have any colour, as long as it's black', when customers enquired about the choice of colour in the Model T range. This clearly illustrates the inflexibility of mass-marketed products.

In practice, the marketing mix has led to a manipulative attitude towards people: 'If we just select the right variables in the right combination and with the right intensity, the consumer will buy; it is a matter of putting pressure on the consumer.'[10] The main problem confronting the marketer was to find an optimal mix that gets a superior response in the market and, at the same time, creates profits.

The manipulative approach to the marketing mix

Management speculates on how to mix the different activities of the marketing mix:

- What will the effect of a certain mix be, and what happens to the other measures if the value of one of them is altered?

- What will happen if we reduce the price by 10 per cent?

- What will happen if we invest more in advertising?

- What will be the effect if we launch a new product for a new segment?

Research was beginning to show that the marketing-mix model of marketing was too restrictive for business-to-business and services marketing. Moreover, it was also becoming an outdated concept for consumer goods marketing, as the importance of intangible service characteristics and customer service considerations became prime differentiating factors among products.[11] It was felt that the marketing mix represented the seller's view of marketing, and it was suggested that marketers should view the 4 Ps from a customer-oriented perspective.

1.3.2 Transactional Marketing

In transactional marketing, the fact that a customer has bought a product does not forecast the probability of another purchase of the same product, not even if a series of purchases has been made. Transactional marketing therefore has no ambition to climb the loyalty ladder. The marketing process ends when the sale has occurred; the sale is the objective and the end result of the marketing effort.[12]

According to the traditional (transactional) marketing concept, the major focus of marketing programmes has been to make customers buy, regardless of whether they are existing or new customers. Often, only a small part of the marketing budget has been allocated directly towards existing customers. Since the 1980s, this approach to marketing has been questioned. It was argued that this approach is no longer broad enough, because of the importance of customer retention, the changes in the competitive environment and the limitations of transactional marketing.[13]

In transactional marketing situations, customers, as unidentified members of a segment, are exposed to a number of competing products, and they are supposed to make independent choices from among the available options. The two parties have conflicting interests. The starting point is that the customer does not *want* to buy; he or she has to be *persuaded* to do so.

Businesses are confronted with many competitive challenges — markets have generally become mature, and there is only limited possibility for product differentiation, therefore customer retention is becoming more important.[14] Thus, transactional marketing is too simplified a framework for today's businesses.

1.3.3 Market Segmentation

According to the marketing concept, the market offering must be focused on satisfying customer needs and preferences optimally. However, marketers have traditionally felt that satisfying individual customer needs is too costly and unrealistic, so they generalise about the needs and preferences of the heterogeneous market. At the same time, marketers feel that they cannot be all things to all people — they must focus on satisfying specific customer needs and concentrate on what they do best to remain competitive in an increasingly competitive marketplace.

The traditional approach to market segmentation focuses on dividing the heterogeneous market into fairly homogeneous sub-sets of customers. Each segment of the market, it is assumed, will have similar needs, and will respond in a similar way to the market offering and strategy. The organisation then has to decide which of the market segments identified it can best satisfy, and develop a product offering and strategy around the needs of that particular segment.[15]

The bases of segmentation that are used are mostly geographic (i.e. dividing the market into different geographical areas), demographic (i.e. using segmentation variables such as income, education and living standards), psychographic (i.e. segmentation by means of categories such as social class, lifestyle and personality) and behavioural (i.e. grouping buyers on the basis of their buying behaviour such as benefits sought, loyalty status and attitude toward the product).

For decades, market segmentation strategies were proving particularly vulnerable, and market segmentation, a central marketing concept, no longer appeared to be operating effectively.[16] While markets were still being presented demographically, geographically and psychographically, the realisation was beginning to dawn on marketers that the only category that was really meaningful was *actual* — as opposed to *speculative* — buyer behaviour. It was therefore becoming increasingly difficult to categorise buyers.

Buyers seem to do unusual things, such as saving their money or deferring spending in some areas and then buying heavily in others. Some customers within a historically defined segment are much more sensitive to some media than others. Some are sensitive to price, others to service. This points to the fact that if the only categorisation that is meaningful is actual buyer behaviour rather than the underlying drivers of that behaviour; then there are no more market segments, but just individual customers.[17] A shift is clearly necessary: from marketing to anonymous masses of customers, to developing and managing relationships with more or less well-known, or at least somehow identifiable, customers.

The recognition of the problems associated with the practice of traditional marketing suggested a crisis in marketing that demanded attention. It was openly debated that a 'paradigm shift' was needed if marketing was going to survive as a discipline.[18]

It was clear that there was a need to transform marketing from a narrow set of functional skills based on the conventional marketing mix to a broader business orientation where delivery of 'superior' customer value was a key objective. In this context, relationship marketing may be a very practical and appropriate approach for marketers to use to regain their edge as the company's strategic driver.

1.4   Relationship Marketing

At least one business rule from the past remains constant: the customer reigns supreme. Successful companies never lose sight of their customers' demands, and are careful to keep track of these needs as they evolve and change.[19]

In the growing theoretical void described so far, the concept of relationship marketing began to take shape across all areas of marketing. The apparent success of a relational approach in the service and business-to-business sectors began to attract the attention of other marketers, who hypothesised the emergence of a new generic marketing paradigm to possibly replace, but certainly augment, the traditional marketing model.[20]

As marketing entered the 1990s, the relationship marketing concept represented a 'new marketing paradigm' — a shift in business thinking — and was regarded as the biggest change in 50 years, in effect taking marketing back to its roots. Relationship marketing became the 'battle cry' of the 1990s.

Relationship marketing is not a wholly independent philosophy, but draws on traditional marketing principles. This view suggests that the basic focus on customer needs still applies, but that it is the *way* marketing is practised that requires changing fundamentally.[21]

One of the first definitions of relationship marketing was the following:[22] Relationship marketing means attracting, maintaining and enhancing customer relationships.

While recognising that customer acquisition was, and would remain, part of a marketer's responsibilities, this viewpoint emphasised that a relationship view of marketing implied that retention and development were more important to the company, in the longer term, than customer acquisition. The most comprehensive definition was proposed by Grönroos:[23]

Definition of relationship marketing

The objectives of relationship marketing are to identify and establish, maintain and enhance, and, when necessary, terminate relationships with customers and other stakeholders at a profit so that the objectives of all parties involved are met. This is done by mutual exchange and fulfilment of promises.

This definition may be seen to include various dimensions that differ significantly from the historical definition of marketing.[24] Let us look at the following dimensions of the definition:

- Relationship marketing (RM) seeks to create new value for customers and then share it with these customers, because customers estimate which offer will deliver the most value, and will buy from the company they perceive as offering the highest perceived value. It was Adam Smith who observed two centuries ago that 'the real price of anything is the toil and trouble of acquiring it; the total cost includes the buyer's time and energy'.[25]

- RM recognises the key role that individual customers have, both as purchasers and in defining the value they wish to achieve.

- RM businesses are seen to design and align processes, communication, technology and people in support of customer value.

- RM represents continuous co-operative effort between buyers and sellers.

- RM recognises the value of customers' purchasing lifetimes (i.e. their lifetime value). Lifetime value stands for the present value of the future profits expected over the customer's lifetime purchases. For example, an American car company estimated that a customer entering its dealership for the first time represents a potential lifetime value of over \$300 000. If the customer is satisfied and buys several cars from the dealership over his or her buying lifetime, this may be the figure (subtracting the cost of selling to and serving the customer). If the satisfied customer brings in other customers, the figure would be higher.

- To create the value customers want, RM seeks to build a chain of relationships within the organisation and between the organisation and its main stakeholders, including suppliers, distribution channels, intermediaries and shareholders.
- One of the main principles of RM is to identify the most profitable customers so that the business can focus on customers appropriate to its strategy.

Figure 1.1 depicts transactional and relationship marketing. Relationship marketing became the new philosophy of marketing. The implementation of this philosophy usually takes place in the popularly known term of customer relationship management (or CRM). However, today many companies realise the importance of CRM, but most companies still operate with a mixture of the transactional marketing and relationship marketing approaches.[26]

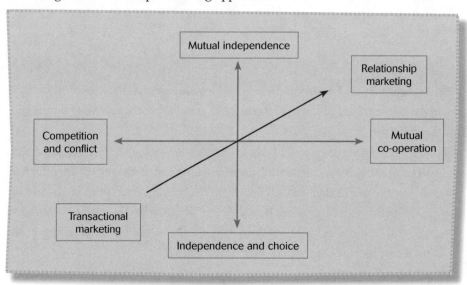

Figure 1.1 Transactional and Relationship Marketing[27]

As illustrated in figure 1.1, the development of relationship marketing points to a significant paradigm shift in marketing: from competition and conflict to mutual co-operation, and from independence and choice to mutual interdependence.

Transactional marketing was rapidly becoming outdated — unsuited to the complex modern marketing reality, with no consideration of future contact with a customer. An organisation thus needs to orient itself toward total customer relationships, as opposed to focusing on single transactions with a customer. This implies the linking of separate transactions, because only this approach enables the utilisation of things such as the cost saving potential of customer retention. If the company does not succeed in continuing and extending relationships based on earlier transactions, a customer will have to be 'newly acquired' prior to each transaction, and the organisation will incur the additional cost of doing this each time.[28]

Relationship marketing is thus the ongoing process of identifying and creating new value with individual customers and then sharing the benefits from this over a lifetime of association. This involves collaboration among supplier and selected customers for mutual value creation.

Let us now look more closely at the focus areas of relationship marketing.

1.5 Focus Areas of Relationship Marketing

The main focus areas that will be dealt with are the individual customer approach (which includes market segmentation and customer lifetime value), and how the traditional marketing mix needs to be reconsidered in terms of relationship marketing.

1.5.1 Individual Customer Approach

One of the key aspects of customer relationship management is to focus on individual customers. In terms of the definition of relationship marketing outlined earlier on, we mentioned that CRM recognises the key role that individual customers have, and the most profitable customers have to be identified so that the business can focus on customers appropriate to its strategy.

Most companies in the 21st century face a radically different competitive landscape. The old economy revolved around manufacturing companies whose main drive was to standardise production, products and business processes.[29] They invested large sums in brand building, while a business was run like a machine.

In the new economy, however, the business is supported by information, which has the ability to differentiate, customise and personalise, and which enables it to gather information about individual customers and business partners such as suppliers. It is thus possible to be more flexible, and the business has the ability to individualise the market offerings, messages and media. The business can thus focus on individual customers, for example:

Focusing on individual customers[30]

 Dell Computers invites customers to specify exactly what they want in a computer and delivers a custom-built one in a few days.

Proctor & Gamble (P&G), on its Reflect.com website, allows someone to specify needs for a shampoo by answering a set of questions. P&G then formulates a unique shampoo for that person.

 Levi's is now able to produce customised jeans that are based on a person's measurements.

Not all customers are the same, thus different customers should be treated differently.[31] The key is to know who the best customers are and to treat them as such. For an organisation that has two million customers, the prospect of cost-effectively communicating, one-to-one, with all of them is an impossible task. Instead, customers should be categorised or segmented, based on what is known about them. These segments can be described and quantified in terms of their value and potential value to an organisation, and appropriate communication strategies can be designed for each segment. Through effective segmentation, for example, a bank manager will know that customers from one particular segment are three times more likely to respond to an investment product offer than customers from any other segment.

A company's success hinges increasingly on using customer-level information and interaction to create long-term, profitable, one-to-one customer relationships. The concept of 'a segment of one' can be seen as a further extension of CRM. In terms of CRM, the marketer should focus on the most profitable customers and reject the unprofitable ones.

Customer knowledge[32]

 To buy a computer, many businesses and consumers now go to the Dell website and order a PC made to their exact specifications. Or they call a rival for similarly mass-customised PCs. And as people come to enjoy customised offerings in some facets of their lives, at prices they are willing to pay, they begin to expect them in other facets as well.

 In the USA, for example, you can now go on the Internet and find any car you want at just a few dollars over dealer prices, or trade 10 000 General Motors shares and pay a commission of less than $8.

 One extreme example is Procter & Gamble, the world's largest producer of packaged consumer goods, who joined forces with Wal-Mart, the world's largest retailer. They have set up an information system that co-ordinates online the production and delivery of the goods with the sales in the stores.

Already the most successful companies in a wide variety of industries are those that have succeeded in developing and maintaining long-term relationships with customers and, more importantly, that embrace the principles of one-to-one marketing — notably Hewlett-Packard, Amazon.com and American Express. These companies have built their success on customer knowledge and interaction.

However, one-to-one marketing is not suitable for every company.[33] Customisation may be very difficult to implement for complex products such as motor cars. It can raise the cost of goods by more than the customer is willing to pay. Some customers do not know what they want until they see actual products. Customers cannot cancel the order after the company has started to work on the product. The product may be hard to repair and have little sales value. In spite of this, customisation has worked well for some products — laptop computers, clothes, skincare products and vitamins.

A business should focus on the most profitable customers and eliminate the unprofitable ones, for example, by encouraging such customers gently but firmly to migrate to competitors. It is felt that customers who are unprofitable today will most probably be unprofitable tomorrow and they do not merit further attention.[34]

One-to-one marketing is basically a simple idea. However, implementing a one-to-one marketing programme is not as simple. In order to build one-to-one relationships, a company must learn continuously from interactions with individual customers, and it must respond dynamically to the information those interactions elicit — it must engage its customers, particularly its best customers, and ensure that they never want to leave.

The question that then arises is: 'How should a market be segmented in terms of CRM?'

1.5.2 Reconsidering Traditional Market Segmentation

In the section above, it was mentioned that market segmentation, as practised for decades, was in need of revision. Firms are experiencing increased pressure to offer customer-centric strategies, because many of their competitors are offering one-to-one or customised marketing strategies. With advances in technology and segmentation methods, segmentation strategies are evolving to reflect this shift in power toward the customer.

Traditionally (see section 1.3.3, above), objectives of segmentation strategies focused on identifying groups of potential customers, for example, profiling prospects for product development, identifying appropriate prospects for marketing campaigns and classifying groups in accordance with the potential response to specific pricing strategies. In terms of CRM, a customer lifetime value (CLV)-based segmentation is a segmentation approach that groups customers into meaningful segments based on customer profitability and lifetime value, and other factors. Moreover, the concepts of customer profitability and CLV are fast becoming accepted as new bases for customer segmentation.[35] CLV enables an organisation to focus on improving the effectiveness of marketing expenditures. For example, using CLV as a basis, a segmentation objective may focus on evaluating customer migration expenditures.

How is customer profitability measured? Many organisations measure customer profitability on the level of sales, the increase in order volume and the size of transactions. Indirect costs (mainly the costs of sales, marketing and general administration) are then allocated across the customer base, often in proportion to the total sales of each customer.[36] (This aspect will be dealt with in greater detail in chapter 2.)

With advances in technology, organisations have access to an abundance of data about their customers, including their purchasing history, attitudinal data collected from customer satisfaction surveys, and demographic and socioeconomic data collected from reward/loyalty programmes.[37] Segmentation offers marketers one approach to utilise this data to customise the organisation's marketing efforts, but successful segmentation efforts require sophisticated models in order to use relevant information and to most effectively target specific customers with appropriate offers to maximise response. In addition, cost-benefit analysis suggests that, in some industries, a CLV segmentation strategy, i.e. clustering customers into meaningful segments based on customer profitability and other variables, may be a more appropriate use of an organisation's resources than individual-level customer profitability models.[38] (In chapter 2 and 8 we will discuss a customer segmentation system that can be used for this purpose.)

CLV looks at what the retained customer is worth to the organisation now, based on the predicted future transactions and costs. Looking forward to the value of future purchases and costs, expressed as the present value of a stream of future profits, fits more comfortably with the development of a relationship marketing approach that is concerned with unlocking value for the organisation and its key customers.[39] Effectively, relationship marketers need to predict the future purchasing behaviour of key customers to arrive at the latter's CLV.

CLV analysis suggests that the value of a relationship with a customer can be increased either by increasing the amount of profit or by extending the relationship lifetime. Customers at the beginning of their relationship lifetime will need a different relationship marketing strategy to those approaching the declining stage of their relationship lifetime. Retail banks understand this principle well; they have identified students as potentially high-value customers over a lifetime, even though in the short term they may be unprofitable.

It is important to remember that customer relationship management is designed to provide increased value to the customer, which ultimately yields a lifetime value to the marketer (service provider).[40] The reason is that higher customer value increases customer satisfaction, thereby instilling customer loyalty, which, in turn, creates higher profit due to increased volume resulting from repeat purchases and positive word of mouth referrals.

Let us now look at how the marketing mix of the traditional marketing approach should be reconsidered in terms of CRM.

1.5.3 Reconsidering the Traditional Marketing Mix[41]

The traditional 4 Ps of marketing, namely product, price, promotion and place/distribution, need to be approached differently according to the new focus on customer relationships. Technology can assist in combining the 4 Ps in numerous variations, thereby offering the customers many choices so that they can obtain precisely what they want (product), when and how they want it (distribution), and at a price that represents the value they wish to receive (price). Technology also enables the company to engage individual customers when and how they wish to communicate (promotion). Thus we can see that technology can assist in digitising the traditional combination of the marketing mix (the 4 Ps), offering the customer many choices. The focus has changed to: It is for the customer to choose, not for the marketer to provide what he/she thinks the customer wants.

By using technology appropriately, an organisation can serve customers as individuals. A data-driven approach enables organisations to assess each customer's needs and potential profitability, and to tailor sales offers and service accordingly. This involves using multiple channels — the Internet, direct mail, telesales and field sales — to improve effectiveness and efficiency. Companies using technology have the potential to be close to the customer and to gain a competitive advantage.

Let us now consider how each of the traditional 4 Ps of marketing should change in RM and CRM terms.

Product

Traditionally, the marketer developed product concepts, researched the customers and then developed the product that would yield the desired profit margin to the business. This never took into account that customers want different things at different times and are often not interested in one standard product or service.

Forcing customers to buy what they do not need

Honda packages anti-lock brakes together with aluminium wheels. If you want one, you must buy the other. The company does not need to do it this way, but it chooses to. Why does Honda force customers to buy aluminium wheels and anti-lock brakes together in a package? The company undoubtedly has different suppliers for wheels and braking systems, so supply factors probably do not drive the packaging. Rather, Honda must have made a conscious management decision, or perhaps something is broken in their internal processes or technologies. This does not mean that Honda does not address customer needs. However, it may indicate an opportunity for Honda to rethink how individual customers are served.

Relationship marketing involves real-time interaction between the company and its priority (most profitable) customers, as it seeks to move more rapidly to meet customer requirements. The customer participates in the development of the product. The product resulting from this collaboration may be unique or highly tailored to the requirements of the customers, with much more of their knowledge content incorporated into the product than was previously the case. Thus, for products and services where the lifetime, volume and margin warrant it, individual customers can and should be considered in every aspect of the business, including the processes that drive new product and service design. This act recognises that customers are not equal — they want different things in different amounts at different times — and the profit derived from each will vary.

In the car industry, when Buick asked the rhetorical question many years ago: 'Can we build one for you?' they did something not done previously by car companies. They went far beyond William Durant's concept of offering cars in a variety of styles and colours that Ford considered impractical, and engineered their processes to enable mass customisation of their vehicles. For the first time, customers could choose features and paid separately for each feature.

Since the 1990s, in another industry, Dell Computer has applied the principle of customer involvement in product specification. Customers choose from among many options, and Dell assembles products as requested by the customer. This, in addition to Dell's innovation in distribution channel directness, has enabled it to become a major contender in a very competitive industry. Consequently, Compaq has announced that it, too, plans to produce to customer order or have computers configured in its dealerships from standard components. Like most computer companies, it previously assembled products in advance, knowing as it did so that it was almost certainly wrong with regard to the numbers it was making and the configuration of some models. Making products according to customer order has a side benefit: total costs can go down as less finished goods inventory becomes obsolete.

Practically, in the near term, management may decide that the costs of full-blown technology implementation cannot be justified economically. However, technology throws down this challenge: if you ignore opportunities to serve customer uniquely using advanced technologies, and your competitors decide to adopt this approach, what will your response be?

Car manufacturers could consider offering customers the following:

- The ability to specify what types of wheels they prefer;

- The flexibility to choose the colour of a particular car, as opposed to being offered a limited range of colours; and

- The opportunity to have a steering wheel customised to suit particular needs.

It is interesting to note that some of the American car manufacturers, such as General Motors, are offering customers the opportunity of ordering customised motorcars, to their exact specifications, on the Internet!

The key challenge for the marketer is to identify the core strategic value that will be delivered to the customer and the elements that the customer can change, allowing the buyer to be firmly in charge, assembling the value he or she wants. For most organisations, mass customisation requires a material shift in current practice — and the marketer can lead the change.

Rethinking products/services

- Some excellent banks in the United States are customising their services to meet the particular needs of their clients. For example, the client assists in designing his/her chequebook, credit card and savings account to meet his/her personal needs. Does this ever happen in South Africa?

General Electric makes jet engines capable of meeting Boeing's specifications. General Electric engines for one type of Boeing plane differ from another, partly because Boeing's knowledge and direction are incorporated in the design and development process.

Price

Traditional marketing sets a price for a product and offers the price of the product in the market. The price seeks to secure a fair return on the investment the company has made in its more-or-less static product.

With relationship marketing, the product varies according to the preferences and dictates of the customers, with the value varying commensurately. So, when customers specify that a product should have specific features and that certain services should be delivered before, during and after the sale, they naturally want to pay for each component of the value bundle separately. Just as the product and services are set in a process of collaboration, so too will the price need to reflect the choices made and the value created from these choices.

Customers want to participate in decisions regarding the value they receive and the prices they pay. Give them a standard offering and they will expect to pay a single price. But offer them options in the product and they will want some more than others, and will pay more for these. Give them a chance to have an even more tailored solution, and they might pay more again. Give them options they don't want, and they will expect these to be removed and deleted from the price.

Relationship marketing, especially in the case of industrial marketing, therefore invites customers into the pricing process and all other value-related processes, giving customers an opportunity to make any desirable trade-offs and to further develop trust in the relationship.

Marketing communication (or promotion)

Traditional marketing uses one-way mass advertising to communicate with customers. This one-way communication, typically employed by marketers with their customers, such as mass advertising, promotional offers, manuals, price lists and warranty response cards, must be replaced with two-way communications to involve the customers much earlier in all matters that affect their future purchase behaviour. Technology can make promotion become *communication*, because technology can engage individual customers when and how they wish to relate. Relationship marketing gives individual customers an opportunity to decide how they wish to communicate with the business.

Customers can be served as individuals by using technology appropriately. With technology, individual end customers can be interactively and uniquely engaged. Using technologies such as the Internet, computer-telephony integration at all centres, intelligence at point-of-sale, smart cards and interactive voice response, companies can give customers a host of options to communicate with the company and have information on hand to engage, inform and direct each customer with complete knowledge as to their preferences.

Distribution (place)

Traditional marketing sees distribution as the channel that takes the product from producer to consumer. For example, in the case of the computer industry, Dell sees distribution as a direct sales approach, primarily using telephone sales and other placement, while IBM uses many approaches to distribution, including its own stores, a direct sales force and retailers that resell the firm's personal computers.

Relationship marketing instead considers distribution from the perspective of the customer who decides where, how and when to buy the combination of products and services that comprise the supplier's total offering. Seen in this way, distribution is not a channel, but a *process*. The process allows customers to choose where and from whom they will obtain the value they want.

> ### Buying a computer the relationship marketing way
>
> The customer can choose whether to buy a computer off the shelf from a reseller and take it home immediately, order one that is built to his/her individual preferences at the factory and shipped within a week or so, or have one that is configured in-store and available within a few days.

It is thus more accurate to think of distribution as a 'placement', using the customers' choice to direct the location at which they will specify, purchase, receive, install, repair and return individual components of the products and services. While traditional marketing considered a product as a bundled package of benefits, relationship marketing unbundles the product and service and allows the customer to initiate a placement decision for each element.

The traditional 4 Ps of Marketing have been extended in recent times to include three additional Ps, namely people, physical evidence and processes. These will be discussed in Chapter 3, as well as their effect on RM and CRM.

Relationship marketing thus offers an opportunity for the company and the marketer to break out of existing frameworks such as the traditional 4 Ps, and to glue the firm into its customers' minds and wallets. It offers marketers a chance to help the company to grow in a competitively challenging environment. Enabled by new technologies, relationship marketing provides the marketer with the tools needed to serve individuals as they wish to be served, throughout their purchasing and consumption lifetimes. Companies that are first to adopt relationship marketing principles in their industries and to apply the concepts with vigour have the potential to gain a first-mover advantage that is difficult for competitors to emulate. Importantly, this means that companies have the potential to gain a pre-emptive position with the best customers and to ensure that the needs of these customers are well addressed long before competitors try to copy and target these same individuals or companies.

One thing has been proved over the last couple of years: CRM, if implemented correctly, means better profits. But before any company can even consider implementing CRM, new capabilities are required to be in place.

1.6 Companies Require New Capabilities

Before embarking on CRM, a company must know who its customers are, their value, what they buy, where they are located and through which channels they want to interact with the company. Management needs to formulate a CRM strategy at all levels, including the people, the business processes, the organisational structure and the technical infrastructure.[42] To implement CRM, the support of top management is essential.

1.6.1 Support at the Executive Level

An organisation wishing to implement CRM must have support at executive level, and there needs to be a commitment to CRM, initiated by top management. In fact, the whole culture of the organisation must change.

The CEO must take the lead and ensure that the message is broadcast throughout the organisation, must understand the real meaning of a relationship before committing the company to CRM and must focus on the value that can be created through relationships with key stakeholders – a value that must be shared by the company and the customer. Also, the most profitable customers to focus on must be identified, and the CEO needs to be strong enough to terminate relationships with unprofitable customers.[43] In some companies, executives try to ensure that they maximise the value of each deal with every customer. However, companies trying to forge relationships with this underlying approach to customers will find that customers have no interest in long-term bonding with such suppliers. The opportunity to create continuously new and mutual value over time will go to competitors more amenable to sharing customers.

Management needs to recognise the fact that the relationship with customers needs to be managed. A relationship manager should work with customers to ensure that they receive the value they seek. Each person within the company communicates and creates value with his/her customer counterpart, with the relationship manager guiding the overall process. In this process, it is necessary to integrate all communications with the customer with the aid of technology.

Without this commitment by top management, CRM cannot succeed. The successful companies in South Africa are those that receive enthusiastic support from customers and who have recognised the importance of adopting CRM as a philosophy behind the business — CRM should be one of an organisation's core values.[44]

What is therefore expected from top management to ensure the successful implementation of customer relationship management? A CEO could consider some of the following actions to create, first of all, a customer-centric approach in the company:[45]

- Convince senior management of the need to become customer focused. Here the CEO personally exemplifies strong customer commitment, and rewards those in the company who do likewise. For example, IBM's top 470 executives are personally responsible for more than 1 300 customer accounts.
- Obtain outside help and guidance. Consulting firms have the experience to help companies move toward a customer orientation.
- Develop strong in-house marketing training programmes for corporate management, divisional managers, marketing and sales personnel, manufacturing personnel and others similar to those run by successful companies such as Motorola and Accenture.
- Establish an annual marketing excellence recognition programme. Reward the winning teams at a special ceremony.
- Shift from a department focus to a process-outcome focus. This means appointing process leaders and cross-disciplinary teams to re-engineer the processes around the customer, and implementing these processes.
- Empower employees. Progressive CEOs empower their employees to settle customer complaints and other problems in order to retain the customer's business. IBM, for example, let its front-line employees spend up to $5 000 to solve a customer problem on the spot.

Study on CRM failure by Accenture[46]

In a recent study by Accenture, the following was found:

- While business executives overwhelmingly agree that technology has helped them strengthen relationships with their customers, the majority say that CRM shortfalls can be attributed in part to inadequate support from top management.

- Many CRM initiatives fail because of the flawed execution of plans, which echoes the view that full potential is achievable by making sure that there is no disconnection between the organisation's vision and its execution.

- CEOs need to take a closer look at innovative and proven methods of maximising the return on investment of CRM and customer value indicatives by going back to basics.

- Too many CRM projects focus on the mechanics, such as technologies, rather than on the ultimate goal, which is to increase the value of the customer relationship.

- Other factors identified explaining the failure of CRM programmes are: the business has no long-term vision; the need for investments is not justified; investments are not prioritised; and return on investment is not calculated.

The next important prerequisite for CRM to be successful is a change in the organisation's processes.

1.6.2 Processes

Process management involves all the procedures, tasks, schedules, mechanisms, activities and routines by which a product or service is delivered to customers. In the traditional functional approach, all business functions operated as silos – i.e. they restricted processes strictly to functional areas, with no interaction with or dependency on other functions of the organisation.

A company wishing to implement CRM needs to manage and link all work processes. High-performance companies are increasingly focusing on the need to manage core business processes such as new product development, customer attraction and retention, and order fulfilment. They are re-engineering work flows and building cross-functional teams responsible for each process.[47] Also, processes should be engineered around the customer, and this often requires essential changes to existing processes; every process should integrate with the customer, thus functional silos are eliminated.

Look at the following examples of high-performing companies that achieve excellent capabilities in managing core business processes through cross-functional teams:

Managing processes by cross-functional teams[48]

- At Xerox, a customer operations group links sales, shipping, installation, service and billing so that these activities flow smoothly into one another.

- Motorola and Polaroid are companies that have reorganised their employees into cross-functional teams.

- A famous zoo changed its organisation. The revamped zoo consists of bioclimatic zones — exhibits that immerse zoo-goers in an environment of predator and prey, and flora and fauna from different parts of the world. Because the zones themselves are more interdependent, the employees who manage them must work together. Gardeners, groundskeepers and animal care experts are no longer separated by traditional boundaries.

Management should focus on building customers into the main processes, and customers should collaborate with management in all the processes that are geared to creating value.[49] For example, communications processes may currently be developed to broadcast to a market segment, when interactive or narrowcast communications may be used instead. Also, the role of the salesperson as historically defined is of value only when new customers are brought on board.

However, when the company is focused on creating value for existing customers, bringing new customers on board has less merit than having the relationship managed in an integrated way by tying together the various processes, people and technologies to which the customer can relate. Product concepts and product design should be developed in close association with the customer mentioned earlier, some banks in the USA, for example, allow customers to design their own cheque books.

Excellent customer service is a further requirement before CRM can be implemented successfully.

1.6.3 Excellent Customer Service[50]

Excellent customer service is an integral part of CRM. No company can even contemplate implementing CRM if it does not offer excellent customer service, which can only be achieved by training *all* employees, e.g. the accounts department, the receptionist, the switchboard operator, the petrol attendant and the salesperson, including even those, such as the back office, who do not have direct contact with customers.

Employees must also understand that their own job satisfaction ultimately rests on the success of the organisation — happy employees make for happy customers. Employees must be supported by technologies and processes to make them more effective. In the traditional marketing era, market and customer knowledge was centralised. Now, in CRM, the people in the front line should have the ability to communicate with customers in a way that recognises them, remembers their contact history, understands current customer issues, predicts anticipated behaviour and suggests appropriate responses or solutions. Front-line employees are becoming consultants, working with customers to add value to their company.

The interaction between employees and customers is referred to as the *service encounter* — this is the actual service the customer receives either face to face, or by telephone, e-mail or through the mail. The service encounter is extremely important for all types of business. Even the interaction between the customer and the provider's service system should be customer friendly, e.g. a bank's interaction between customer and ATM or Internet bank. Unfriendly systems scare customers away.

For example, a customer calling to enquire about the operation of a new product should be met by someone who has the appropriate information. The information will come either directly from that person, or indirectly from data warehouses or people with the knowledge, which will require that the person be able to engage new processes to access, assess and communicate the information. Customer service will be dealt with comprehensively in chapter 3.

A superior service encounter

Some credit card companies have an unsurpassed ability to handle customer information. Suppose a customer calls to cancel his or her card because of the high interest charged by the credit card company. The Intelligent Call Routing System immediately displays three counteroffers of interest rates from 12.9 to 9.9 per cent. The representative has the power to negotiate a new interest rate with the customer in an effort to pre-empt the cancellation of the credit card, and is eligible for a bonus, depending on the outcome of the negotiation.

Disneyland: Superior service[51]

The staff at Disneyland is either on- or offstage. Onstage, everyone participates in a show, regardless of whether they are actors in the traditional sense, sell tickets, serve hamburgers or pick up litter. Consequently, everyone knows their part, and this creates satisfied customers. One of the ten commandments of Disneyland says: 'We're on stage and we know our role in the show. We're entertainers, we know our "script", we know our standards and we never miss a cue. We consistently give a good show — all the time.'

1.6.4 Technology to Gain Customer Knowledge and Insight

Once customer-centricity has been established in an organisation, technology enables it to acquire knowledge about customers, establish a database and gain insight into this knowledge through data mining. Only once all these have been accomplished should the organisation implement a CRM system.

CRM is technology driven, but technology is only the enabler. By using technology appropriately, an organisation can serve customers as individuals. However, technology is merely the facilitator of CRM and does not solve all problems a business may have.

Let us look at what should be achieved before a CRM system is acquired:

- **First establish customer-centricity:** Before any organisation decides to deploy CRM technology, it must first include customer-centricity as part of its corporate vision and mission.[52] Customer-centricity requires a focus on the primacy of the customer, whereas previously the focus may have been on marketing strategies designed to promote the sales of specific products or services.

Technology in CRM[53]

- CRM is a strategic initiative, not an IT initiative. It is a strategy that requires fundamental changes within an organisation: the organisation needs to become customer-centric, business processes need to change and a solution needs to be defined that will support all these changes.

- Many organisations are operating on the principle that technology is the answer to all its problems. The reality is that technology is only ever as good as the people who operate the systems. Ninety-five per cent of technological systems show no return, and, in fact, use up resources, simply because the people operating those systems have not been trained to optimise their benefits.

- CRM is not about having a fancy database, but about how knowledge is leveraged (used) to optimise a business and ensure long-term client relations to the benefit of all stakeholders.

Develop a database: Once the concept of customer primacy has been established, the task of how to weave the various databases required to support this primacy into a comprehensive whole, and then to manage it, comes to the fore. CRM systems must be capable of integrating all knowledge about key customers into valuable business intelligence in real time through any channel. This business intelligence is the key to unlocking real value for a CRM strategy.

Successful companies are capturing information every time a customer comes into contact with any of its departments. The contact points include a customer purchase, a customer-requested service call, an online query or a mail-in rebate card. This data is collected by the company's contact centre and organised into a data warehouse. Company personnel can then capture, query and analyse the data. Inferences can then be drawn about an individual customer's needs and responses.

In this way, a unified view of the customer is achieved, which enables any employee to access all information pertinent to a client, from his/her purchasing history to his/her service record and credit rating.[54]

Use data mining to predict: Through data mining, marketing statisticians can extract useful information about individuals, trends and segments from the mass of data. Data mining involves the use of sophisticated statistical techniques such as cluster analysis and predictive modelling, in order to:[55]

◆ identify prospects;

◆ decide which customers should receive a particular offer;

◆ deepen customer loyalty;

◆ reactivate customer purchases; and

◆ avoid serious customer mistakes.

For this purpose, a company needs a suitable CRM system.

Acquire a suitable CRM system: This requires a large investment. Integrating multiple customer interaction channels with customer service operations, existing enterprise applications and external business suppliers can be complex, time-consuming and expensive.[56] A CRM solution must support all channels of customer interaction and connect easily with all of a company's front- and back-office enterprise applications, and with its other business functions, as well as with those of its external suppliers and business partners. Building on the automation of functions and integration of back-end processes, companies must create central repositories of customer data from which they can extract knowledge about their clients, which they can translate into appropriate action.

To ensure appropriate, relevant use of customer data, companies need databases that integrate customer information and business intelligence across every point of customer interaction and across every business function.

CRM systems help define these collaborative processes. CRM software involves every business process both inside and outside a business. It aligns business processes for customer-centricity, increases corporate revenues and profits, and brings considerable competitive advantage. Most organisations have spent significant portions of their budget resources on IT. Some will have worked, some not.

One of the main difficulties companies experience with their customer database is that employees in the company find it difficult to become customer-oriented and use the available information, and thus find it difficult to practise CRM.

But with a properly developed CRM strategy, a CRM-trained salesperson making a pitch for new business to an existing customer will be aware of any service problems the customer has encountered and can appear to have taken ownership of the solution. Armed with a track record of previous purchases and customer service problems, a service department could turn problem resolution into an opportunity to cross- or up-sell.

By linking together data related to back-office functions, such as accounts, with the front office, organisations can track products through the delivery cycle, providing customers with up-to-date information about their ability to fulfil orders.

To have the required customer knowledge, an organisation thus needs an infrastructure of technology that captures, stores and processes data needed to derive customer knowledge, and an architecture of the technology that places customer data at its strategic heart. Companies should thus focus on gaining customer knowledge and insight and then using this to deepen and extend customer relationships.[57]

1.6.5 The Value of CRM Capabilities

One may ask an important question now: How much are these CRM capabilities worth to a company? Research indicates that the most profitable companies develop a very specific set of CRM capabilities. Conversely, those that do not invest in building these specific capabilities leave millions of rand in profit on the table. But technology is only the enabler and will not do the job for you. Each business must reinvent itself to really produce CRM benefits. The world's leading business software suppliers have also reinvented themselves to focus on CRM.

CRM capabilities increase profit[58]

In one study, it was found that a typical one billion rand business could add

R40–50 million in profit by enhancing specific CRM capabilities by just 10 per cent, whereas companies that achieve the highest level of CRM performance could improve their pre-tax profit by as much as R120–140 million.

Anderson Consulting survey[59]

In a study by Anderson Consulting, it was found that companies that enjoy the highest profitability are those that have invested in developing CRM capabilities. Twenty-one such CRM capabilities were identified: topping the list was motivating and rewarding employees, followed by excellence in delivering customer service, turning customer information into insight, attracting and retaining the right personnel, and building selling and service skills. The influence of technology accounted for about 40 per cent of CRM's impact and will become important with the rapid growth of e-commerce.

The survey further indicated that the highest-performing companies gave front-line employees quick and easy access to critical customer information. And top performers even shared this information with channel partners outside their organisation.

The end result of establishing a relationship with the profitable customers is customer loyalty and, ultimately, greater profitability.

1.7 Summary

One business rule from the past has remained constant: the customer reigns supreme. Successful companies never lose sight of their customers' demands, and are careful to keep track of their customers' needs as they evolve and change.

A company can attract and retain customers by knowing and delivering what they want, when they want it, how they want it, and making it easy and problem-free for customers to interact with the organisation. Thus CRM solutions have become strategic requirements in a customer-focused economy. These solutions can help organisations attract and retain customers in highly competitive markets.

Discussion Questions

1. Explain how customer relationship management has evolved from the marketing concept.

2. Explain and illustrate why traditional marketing practices are not so relevant any more in the modern business world.

3. How do relationship marketing and customer relationship management solve the problems that are encountered with the traditional approach to marketing?

4. An organisation wishing to implement CRM needs to change many of the old traditional approaches of marketing, and it also requires new capabilities that can be considered as prerequisites for the implementation of CRM. In light of this statement, explain these prerequisites or new capabilities for CRM.

5. In a nutshell, what does the individual customer approach entail?

6. Explain the concepts of customer profitability and customer lifetime value (CLV).

Mini Case Study[60]

Toyota: Continuous improvement and mass customisation

For three decades, Toyota enlisted its employees in a relentless drive to find faster, more efficient methods to develop and make low-cost, defect-free cars. The results were stupendous. Toyota became the benchmark in the car industry for quality and low cost.

The same, however, cannot be said for mass customisation, Toyota's latest pioneering effort. With US companies finally catching up, Toyota's top managers set out in the late 1980s to use their highly skilled, flexible workforce to make varied and often individually customised products at the same low cost as standardised, mass-produced goods. They saw this approach as a more advanced stage of continuous improvement.

By 1992, Toyota seemed to be well on its way to achieving its goals of lowering its new product development time to 18 months, offering customers a wide range of options for each model, and manufacturing and delivering a made-to-order car within three days.

However, Toyota ran into trouble and had to retreat, at least temporarily, from its goal of becoming a mass customiser. As production costs soared, top managers widened product development and model life cycles, and asked dealers to carry more inventory. After Toyota's investigations revealed that

20 per cent of the product varieties accounted for 80 per cent of the sales, it reduced its range of offerings by one fifth.

What happened? Many answers to this question have been put forward, but according to Toyota top managers, they had learned the hard way that mass customisation is not simply continuous improvement plus. Continuous improvement is a prerequisite for mass customisation; however, continuous improvement and mass customisation require very different organisational structures, values, management roles and systems, learning methods and ways of relating to customers.

One of the main causes of the problems was that while Toyota had been pursuing mass customisation, it had retained the structures and systems of continuous improvement organisations. Also, like mindless continuous improvers, engineers created technically elegant features, regardless of whether customers wanted the additional choices. In mass customisation, customer demand drives model varieties.

Questions

1. Identify all the mistakes made by Toyota in its pioneering effort with regard to mass customisation, and make suggestions on how to rectify them.

2. Explain to Toyota the ways in which the company should have changed in order to implement mass customisation, or simply CRM.

References

1   Egan, J. 2001. *Relationship Marketing*. Harlow: Pearson Education, pp. 11–13.
2   Doyle, P. 1995. Marketing in the new millennium. *European Journal of Marketing*, 29 (12), p. 23.
3   Gummesson, E. 2002. *Total Relationship Marketing*. Oxford: Butterworth-Heinemann, p. 14.
4   Mattsson, LG. 1997. *Relationships in a Network Perspective: Relationships and Networks in International Markets*. Oxford: Elsevier, p. 37.
5   Gordon, IH. 1998. *Relationship Marketing*. Toronto: John Wiley, p. 37.
6   Drucker, P. 1954. *The Practice of Management*. New York: Harper & Row, p. 36.
7   Gummesson, *op. cit.*, p. 14.
8   Buttle, FB. 1996. *Relationship Marketing Theory and Practice*. London: Paul Chapman, p. 7.
9   Gordon, *op. cit.*, p. 47.
10 Gummesson, *op. cit.*, p. 285.
11 Egan, *op. cit.*, p. 14.

12   Brink, A, Strydom, JW, Machado, R & Cant, MC. 2001. *Customer Relationship Management Principles.* Pretoria: Unisa, p. 4.

13   Hollensen, S. 2003. *Marketing Management: A Relationship Approach.* Harlow: Financial Times/Prentice-Hall, p. 12.

14   *Ibid.*, p. 14.

15   Based on Cant, MC. 2004. *Essentials of Marketing.* Cape Town: Juta, pp. 154–58.

16   Egan, *op. cit.*, p. 17.

17   Gordon, *op. cit.*, p. 5.

18   Grönroos, C. 1994. From marketing mix to relationship marketing: Towards a paradigm shift in marketing. *Management Decisions*, 32 (2), pp. 4–20.

19   Kotler, P. 2003. *Marketing Management.* Upper Saddle River: Prentice-Hall, pp. 26–27.

20   Egan, *op. cit.*, p. 17.

21   Christopher, M. 1996. From brand values to customer values. *Journal of Marketing Practice*, 2 (1), pp. 55–66.

22   Berry, LL. 1983. Relationship marketing. In Berry, LL, Shostack, GL & Upsay, GD. *Emerging Perspectives on Service Marketing.* Chicago: American Marketing Association, pp. 25–28.

23   Grönroos, *op. cit.*, pp. 4–20.

24   Gordon, *op. cit.*, p. 9.

25   Kotler, *op. cit.*, p. 60.

26   Hollensen, *op. cit.*, p. 11.

27   *Ibid.*

28   Osarenkhoe A & Bennani, A. 2007. An exploratory study of implementation of customer relationship management strategy. *Business Process Management Journal*, 13 (1), pp. 139–64.

29   Kotler, *op. cit.*, p. 36.

30   Brink *et al.*, *op. cit.*, pp. 17, 63.

31   Peppers, D, Rogers, N & Dorf, B. 1999. *One to One Fieldbook.* New York: Currency Doubleday, p. 1.

32   Gordon, *op. cit.*, p. 6.

33   Kotler, *op. cit.*, p. 37.

34   Brink *et al.*, *op. cit.*, pp. 54–59.

35   Lemon, KN & Mark, T. 2006. Customer lifetime value as the basis of customer segmentation: Issues and challenges. *Journal of Relationship Marketing*, 5 (2/3), pp. 55–61.

36   Ryals, LJ. 2002. Are your customers worth more than money? *Journal of Retailing and Consumer Services*, 9, pp. 241–51.

37   Kolko, J & Gazala, ME. 2005. *Demystifying Segmentation.* Boston: Forrester Research.

38   Libai, B, Narayandas, D & Humby, C. 2002. Toward an individual customer profitability model. *Journal of Service Research*, 5 (1), pp. 69–76.

39   Ryals, LJ & Knox, S. 2005. Measuring risk-adjusted customer lifetime value and its impact on relationship marketing strategies and shareholder value. *European Journal of Marketing*, 39 (5/6), pp. 456–72.

40 Liu, BS, Petruzzi, NC & Sudharshan, D. 2007. A service effort allocation model for assessing customer lifetime value in service marketing. *Journal of Services Marketing*, 21 (1), pp. 24–35.

41 Based on Brink, A. 2004. *Customer Relationship Management Principles.* Unisa: Centre for Business Management.

42 De Jager, R. 2000. Implementation can affect every aspect of a business. *Business Day* survey, 7 August, p. 15.

43 Gordon, *op. cit.*, pp. 23–24.

44 Brunjes, B & Roderick, R. 2002. Customer relationship management: Why it does and does not work in South Africa. Paper presented at the IMM conference, Johannesburg, p. 10.

45 Kotler, *op. cit.*, p. 679.

46 Accenture. 2002. *Computing SA*, 22 (26), 15 July, p. 13.

47 Kotler, *op. cit.*, pp. 66–67.

48 Nevens, TM, Summe, GL & Uttal, B. 1990. Commercializing technology: What the best companies do. *Harvard Business Review*, p. 162.

49 Gordon, *op. cit.*, p. 31.

50 Brink *et al.*, *op. cit.*, pp. 20–30.

51 Gummesson, *op. cit.*, p. 199.

52 Brink, A. 2003. Customer relationship management: Battle cry of the 1990s. Presentation at the conference on Customer Relationship Management in the Public Sector, January, p. 4.

53 The *Future of Customer Relationship Management*, 1, October 1999.

54 Brink, *op. cit.*, p. 12.

55 Kotler, *op. cit.*, pp. 54–55.

56 *Ibid.*, p. 56.

57 Brink *et al.*, *op. cit.*, pp. 67–69.

58 Accenture. n.d. The view from the top: What every CEO should know. <http://www.accenture.com>.

59 Coetzer, J. 2000. Strategy important, but execution the key. *Business Day* survey, p. 15.

60 Gilmore, JH & Pine, BJ. 2000. *Markets of One.* Boston: Harvard Business School Publishing, pp. 149–50.

C H A P T E R

2

Building Customer Relationships

2.1 Introduction

Think for a moment what it will be like to get into your car in just a few years from now. The car will automatically recognise you by your weight and then adjust all the comfort items to your liking, such as seat height and angle, air-conditioning, mirrors and radio settings. The car sets its shocks at a level that will return a real feel for the road, because that is how you like to drive. As you drive, the car notes and remembers how you start and stop; how you turn, accelerate and brake. Fuel flow and timing are adjusted so that the engine performs as economically and responsibly as possible for your personal driving habits, in daylight or at night, on dry roads or wet, in the city or on the highway. If you want to change your comfort settings, you announce to the car, 'This is the way I like it,' or, 'Set my seat this way when I'm wearing high heels.'

There is a strong link between an individual customer and a car that remembers its driver. It is similar to the link between an interactive grocery delivery service and the shopper whom it reminds to check his or her supply of paper towels, based on his or her previous purchases. Each is an example of a learning relationship. Customer relationship management focuses on building up a learning customer relationship, developing a base of loyal customers and at the same time increasing profitability.

> ### Focus on customer relationships[1]
>
> Forward-thinking organisations realise the importance of knowing customers and understanding their lifetime value. Goods and services are no longer sufficient to differentiate organisations. Rather, customers are increasingly making purchase decisions based on a perception of their relationship with a particular organisation.

This chapter is about customer relationships and how to build them. We will explore the nature of a learning relationship and how to improve it. We will also look at which relationships are not realistic, and the stages in relationship development. We will explore customer retention, which is a prerequisite for relationship loyalty; the lifetime value of a customer; and its implications for profitability.

2.2 The Learning Relationship

To improve a customer relationship, the marketer needs to acquire knowledge about the customer and be able to develop insight into this knowledge, and also to interact regularly with the customer to acquire new information.

2.2.1 Learning Relationships Are Built on Knowledge

A learning relationship between a customer and an organisation gets smarter and smarter with every individual interaction, defining in ever more detail the customer's own individual needs and tastes.[2] The more customers teach Company C, the better it becomes at providing exactly what they want, and the more difficult it will be for a competitor to entice them away.[3] Even if a competitor were to build exactly the same capabilities, a customer already involved in a learning relationship with Company C would have to spend an inordinate amount of time and energy teaching the competitor what Company C already knows. Thus a powerful competitive advantage has been created by Company C.

> ### A learning relationship
>
> Every time a customer orders her groceries by calling up last week's list and updating it, for instance, she is in effect 'teaching' the grocery shopping delivery service more about the products she buys and the rate at which she consumes them. The shopping service will develop a knowledge of this particular customer that is virtually impossible for a competitive shopping service to duplicate, providing an impregnable lock on the customer's loyalty.

In order to have knowledge of customers, as well as insight into this knowledge, it is, of course, necessary to obtain information. This information is then used to create a database for the customer, which becomes the foundation for subsequent CRM activities. Technology enables companies to gather and store information about every individual customer in a sophisticated customer database. After you have bought a new car, for example, the dealer could use a database with information about your purchase, as well as your personal needs and preferences. After a year or two, he or she could contact you to enquire if you are thinking of buying a new car. Thus, companies that focus on gaining customer knowledge and developing insight into this knowledge can deepen and extend customer relationships. The database of a supermarket, for example, should ideally contain the following information:[4]

- **transactions:** a complete history of the purchases made by the customer, including the purchase date, the price paid and whether or not the merchandise was purchased in response to a special promotion or marketing activity;
- **customer contacts:** a record of the interactions that the customer has had with the store, including visits to the website and enquiries made by telephone, plus information initiated by the retailer, such as direct mail sent to the customer;

- **customer preferences:** what the customer likes, such as favourite colours, brands, fabrics and flavours, as well as clothes sizes;
- **descriptive information:** demographic data (e.g. age, income) and psychographic data (e.g. lifestyle, social class) describing the customer that can be used to develop market segments; and
- **responses to marketing activities:** the analysis of the transaction and contact data provides information about the customer's responsiveness to marketing activities.

The customer database can provide important information for planning, e.g. merchandise assortment in a store, provided that the necessary insight into this knowledge can be developed.

A database provides insight into knowledge

A supermarket chain that sells over 300 types of cheese may find that feta cheese is ranked 295th in sales. This may suggest that feta should not get a good location in the cheese department and might even be a candidate for elimination from the assortment. However, further analysis may uncover that feta cheese ranks 25th in sales for the supermarket's best customers. This would mean not eliminating it from the assortment, and it may require a different marketing activity than originally suggested by the low ranking.

Whereas traditional marketing tended to regard information as a source of power, learning relationships imply that information is a valuable resource in building relationships. Because of the competitive advantage based on knowledge about customers, a company that can cultivate learning relationships with its customers should be able to retain their business virtually forever, provided that it continues to supply high-quality customised products or services at reasonably competitive prices and does not miss the next technology wave. Learning relationships would not have saved an ox wagon manufacturer from the motorcar!

Most relevant knowledge comes not only from customers, but through and with them. Increasingly, companies are recognising that they should work *with* their customers in joint knowledge-creating processes to develop deep bonding and a more informed capability to respond to customers.

2.2.2 Customer Interaction Enhances Relationships

Interacting with a customer to learn how satisfied the customer is, or whether the customer has an unspoken complaint, is really just another way of obtaining information about that customer's needs.[5] What the organisation wants to know is how to make the service better for that customer at the next opportunity. If a company can find out how to treat a specific customer better the next time it has dealings with him/her, it can begin to lock that customer into a learning relationship with it. If, every time a customer deals with you, it is more satisfying for that customer than it was the previous time, you are creating a learning relationship with the customer, and, after just a few interactions, the customer will become very loyal. However, this type of interaction should not be used in excess, otherwise the customer will begin to resist interacting at all. One good principle to apply is to check on a customer's satisfaction whenever anything out of the ordinary has occurred in the relationship, e.g. a particularly large purchase such as a car, or a problem in financing.

Let us look at some rules of engagement that should be kept in mind when interacting with customers:

Rules of engagement[6]

- Do not initiate an interaction with a customer without a clear objective.
- Do not ask a customer the same thing more than once.
- Interact in the medium of the customer's choice.
- When engaging in an interaction, start with the customer, not the product.
- Make the interaction personal and personalised.
- Ensure that your interactions with customers are always welcomed.
- Protect the customer's privacy.
- Invite dialogue by printing toll-free numbers and website URLs on everything.
- Ensure that the customer can see the value of each interaction.
- Be sensitive to the customer's time; do not try to learn everything about a customer all at once.

As technology has made interactions increasingly less costly, businesses are finding that they can afford to interact with a wider range of customers economically. Technology also allows an organisation to streamline and automate many of the manual interactions required in serving customers, thus reducing costs and saving time, often quite dramatically. Consider the following example:[7]

Ford: Interacting with customers

Ford Motor Company developed a website for its car owners. In addition to making it easier for customers to communicate with Ford and its dealers, the web-based service Ford offered included configuration and pricing of new car purchases, financing and leasing services, and documentation of each car's service history. One problem Ford still has, like other car companies, is finding out exactly when a customer is 'in the market' for a new car. This is 'strategic value' information. While there are statistical techniques for making gross estimates as to when a particular person might be in the market for a new car, the only reliable way to know is to ask the customer directly. To do this, however, Ford (and all other companies) first has to create a cost-efficient mechanism for supporting the dialogue, as well as a relationship with the customer that is already based on regular interaction.

As most companies attempt to establish relationships with their customers, they should bear in mind that in some cases there are reasons why attempting to develop a relationship may be a fruitless pursuit, because some relationships are simply unrealistic.[8]

2.3 Unrealistic Relationships

It is not possible for all types of businesses to apply learning relationships, because there are no powerful benefits to be gained from some relationships. Some customers may not be suitable for the investment needed in developing a relationship, as it may prove to be too costly. Frequently, there may be a need to change an organisation's marketing activities and increase the marketing expenditure on the relationship-building elements of the marketing mix. Marketers therefore need to consider the potential lifetime value of a customer and determine whether it is appropriate to make this commitment. When is a learning relationship therefore appropriate?

There are many situations where relationship development is unrealistic, from either the customer's or the supplier's point of view. For example, it may just not be a viable proposition for a supplier to embark on costly relationship-building strategies, or there may be no reason why the seller would ever see the buyer again.

Appropriate relationships[9]

Companies such as home builders, real estate brokers and appliance manufacturers — which do not interact frequently with end users of their products — cannot learn enough to make a learning relationship with those customers work. But they might find it beneficial to develop such relationships with general contractors.

Makers of products such as paper clips, whose revenue or profit margin per customer is too low to justify building individual learning relationships with customers, might find it advantageous to cultivate learning relationships with office-supply chains, which interact directly with end users of their products.

A number of unrealistic customer scenarios exist, and these include:[10]

- where there is no reason why, or little likelihood that, a buyer will purchase again from a supplier. A buyer who is unlikely ever to patronise a supplier will see no benefit from establishing a relationship and may indeed be annoyed by the tactics associated with it, such as data capture;

- where buyers want to avoid a relationship, as it may lead to a dependency on a seller. This situation may exist when any benefits associated with the relationship are outweighed by lost opportunities elsewhere;

- where buying processes are formalised in a way that prevents either party developing relationships based on social bonds. Formalised buying situations may be compromised and jeopardised by too close an association between buyer and seller (e.g. those involving government agencies); and

- where the costs associated with a relationship put the buyer at a cost disadvantage in a price-sensitive market. It may be more profitable for buyers in certain markets to keep their eyes open for the best deal available, rather than narrow the field and commit themselves to one supplier. Indeed, they may well prefer to play suppliers off against one another using an organisation's potential insecurity to gain added value.

Certain requirements for a relationship will also indicate whether CRM strategies should be considered. These requirements are essential ingredients for a relationship to be successful.

2.4   Essential Ingredients of a Relationship

The success of a business relationship lies in the development and growth of trust and commitment among partners. The two parties also need to have shared goals and mutual benefits to build a successful relationship.

2.4.1 Trust and Commitment

The presence of relationship commitment and trust is central to successful CRM. Consequently, interactions that lack these two elements do not develop into relationships.[11] According to the Commitment-Trust Theory of Relationship Marketing, relationships exist through the retention of trust and commitment; thus, when both commitment and trust are present — not just one or the other — they produce outcomes that promote efficiency, productivity and effectiveness.[12]

Trust

Trust is seen as an expression of confidence between parties in the exchange that will not be harmed or put at risk by either party's actions. Thus, trust is *the willingness to rely on an exchange partner in whom one has confidence*; it is a generalised expectancy held by an individual that the word of another can be relied upon. These descriptions of trust highlight the importance of confidence, i.e. the firm belief that the trustworthy party is reliable and has high integrity, and are associated with such qualities as consistency, competence, honesty, fairness, responsibility, helpfulness and benevolence.

There would appear to be considerable overlap between trust and satisfaction, as they both represent an overall evaluation, feeling or attitude about the other party in a relationship. Satisfaction may be developed through personal experience or, less directly, through opinion and the experience of peers. It is associated with the perceived standard of delivery and may well be dependent on the duration of the relationship. We can therefore say that high levels of service need to be present throughout the product service delivery process. This would enable customers to receive what they want, when they want it — a perfect delivery each and every time with the desired levels of service that appeal to the consumer. This, in turn, may motivate customer retention. Further, satisfaction over a long period of time reinforces the perceived reliability of the firm and contributes to trust; and anticipated levels of satisfaction may also have an important effect on the duration of the trust.[13]

To build trust is to ensure that customers know that the business will stand behind its promise of service and honour its commitments. In the service sector, for example, trust is particularly relevant, because customers often do not buy services as such. What they buy are implicit and explicit promises of service, e.g.:

- promises that insurance companies will honour future claims;
- promises that banks will correctly process cheques; and
- promises that home security systems will promptly contact the police when burglars break in.

Trust is therefore an important element of a relationship-building programme, because it builds confidence, fosters cooperation, and gives the service provider a second chance when inevitable mishaps occur. It may not be possible to rebuild customer relationships when trust is broken.

Trust is a major determinant of relationship commitment.

Commitment

Commitment is undoubtedly connected with the notion of trust. Commitment can be defined as *an enduring desire to maintain a valued partnership*.[14] Commitment implies that both parties will be loyal, reliable and show stability in their relationship with one another. It is, therefore, a desire to maintain a relationship often indicated by ongoing investment into activities that are expected to maintain that relationship. As it may take time to reach a point where a commitment may be made, it may also imply a certain 'maturity' in a relationship.

Trust facilitates commitment to a relationship, because commitment creates a sense of vulnerability, but this risk is reduced with trust. One exchange partner accepts a lower immediate return with the expectation that their exchange partner will allow them a larger future benefit. Buyers and sellers who accept the premise of an unequal exchange benefit with parity being achieved over time will seek trust-based relationships and will partner only with trustworthy partners. Trust reduces the perception of vulnerability, because it reduces the expectation that a partner would engage in opportunistic behaviour while increasing confidence that short-term inequalities will be equalised over time.[15]

Therefore, when both commitment and trust are present, they produce outcomes that promote efficiency, productivity and effectiveness. In short, commitment and trust lead directly to cooperative behaviours that are conducive to relationship marketing success.

In a business relationship, excellent customer service is, of course, a major prerequisite. Some customers are known to have said, 'Stop sending the birthday cards — just answer the phone the first time!'

A relationship is further sustained through the same shared values, together with relationship benefits.

2.4.2 Shared Goals and Mutual Benefits

Shared goals and mutual benefits are also key factors in building effective business relationships. The extent to which the partners have beliefs in common about behaviours, goals and policies that are important, appropriate and right for a particular situation is likely to affect commitment to a relationship.[16]

The existence of shared goals has been found to have significant effects on relationships that could be profoundly useful to the sellers of products and services.[17] People with shared goals expect to receive help from each other; they share relevant information, and trust the information that they receive, because it is in the interests of both sides to maximise their joint effectiveness and their joint goal attainment.

In contrast to what has been said about factors such as trust and commitment being essential ingredients of a relationship, absence of commitment to a relationship is, however, possible in workable relationships, as illustrated in the following example:

Relationships with no trust and commitment

In the retailing sector, consumers have no reason to commit themselves to one or a few retailers, because of the availability of a large supply of retailers in a largely undifferentiated market. What at first might appear to be 'commitment' on the part of consumers may hide the fact that they have few other exchange possibilities and are 'trapped' rather than committed to the relational exchange.

The irony is that the retailing sector, where commitment is low, is the industry most heavily involved in 'loyalty schemes'. If commitment is a rarity in these businesses, then loyalty is also in short supply. Indeed, most loyalty schemes, while rewarding repeat behaviour, are little more than technically advanced promotions that have little to do with retention, and may actively work against the development of long-term commitment.

Uncommitted customers will be attracted by the best deal with little regard to who supplies it. Once a better brand appears, the consumer will easily switch to another supplier, as there is no trust and commitment.

As mentioned earlier, the purpose of building relationships with customers is to retain customers. And by retaining customers, loyalty is created; and loyalty, in turn, results in superior long-term financial performance. So let us explore relationship loyalty in more detail.

2.5 Relationship Loyalty

Loyalty is a concept close to the heart of customer relationship management. To fully understand relationship loyalty, it is necessary to look at loyalty in perspective – to explore customer retention as well as customer migration, customer bonding strategies and the lifetime value of customers.

2.5.1 Customer Loyalty in Perspective

Customer loyalty, the objective of CRM, is more than having customers make repeat purchases, and being satisfied with their experiences and products or services they purchased. Customer loyalty means that customers are committed to purchasing products and services from a specific organisation, and will resist the activities of competitors attempting to attract their patronage. They have a bond with the organisation, and the bond is based on more than a positive feeling about the organisation.

> **Loyalty towards a retailer**[18]
>
> Loyal customers have an emotional connection with the retailer. Their reasons for continuing to patronise the retailer go beyond the convenience of the retailer's store or the low prices and specific brands offered. They feel such goodwill toward the retailer that they will encourage their friends and family to buy from it.

Loyalty can be defined as the *'biased behavioural response, expressed over time by customers with respect to one supplier out of a set of suppliers, which is a function of decision making and evaluative processes resulting in brand or store commitment'*.[19] Simple patronage, therefore, is not enough. Loyalty, if it is to be genuine, must be seen as biased repeat purchase behaviour, or repeat patronage accompanied by a favourable attitude.

Many companies, having secured a customer's order, turn their attention to seeking new customers without understanding the importance of maintaining and improving the relationships with their existing customers. Too little emphasis is therefore placed on generating repeat business. The objective of relationship marketing is to turn new customers into regularly purchasing customers, and then progressively to move them through being strong supporters of the company and its product, and finally to being active and vocal advocates for the company, thus playing an important role as a referral source. And in this process, customer service has a pivotal role to play in achieving this progression up the ladder of customer loyalty.[20]

Developing customer loyalty is not a question of making 'un-loyal' customers loyal.[21] Some customers will never be loyal to you or to your competitors, and you must accept this. However, you can make sure that you keep your existing customers loyal by giving them more reasons to stay loyal. You can also encourage uncommitted customers to become more loyal, and, by profiling the types of customers who are loyal, you can actively seek other customers who have similar profiles. The retention of loyal customers is of great importance to any organisation.

One of the key elements of customer retention is customer satisfaction. As a rule, the more satisfied the customer, the more durable the relationship. And the longer this lasts, the more money the company stands to make.

There are a number of techniques for measuring customer satisfaction and linking them directly to corporate profitability. The simplest, yet one of the most effective, is 'customer retention', where satisfaction is measured by the rate at which customers are kept – the 'customer retention rate'. This is expressed as the percentage of customers at the beginning of the year that still remain at the end of the year. The more satisfied the customers are, the longer they stay and thus the higher the retention rate. A retention rate of 80 per cent means that, on average, customers remain loyal for five years, whereas one of 90 per cent pushes the average loyalty period up to ten years. And as the average 'life' of a customer increases, so does the profitability of that customer to the company.[22]

Ways of retaining customers will be dealt with under loyalty strategies in chapter 8.

2.5.2 Customer Retention

Many companies spend a great deal of effort, time and money wooing new customers, yet surprisingly few take equal trouble to retain existing customers.[23] Very few companies actually go to the trouble of regularly measuring customer

Customer bonding at banks[24]

Banks in South Africa probably devote most of their resources and energy to attracting new customers, but few take the trouble to retain existing ones. This, of course, is changing, but one wonders whether South African banks will truly adopt the strategies of CRM or whether they will merely pay lip service to the theory. In the last decade, the emphasis was on quality, and quality service in particular, and, while banks certainly attempted to focus on these issues in training and other strategies, little impact in terms of excellent customer service has been felt by the average banking customer.

satisfaction in any systematic way, partly because they are obsessed by a perceived need to win new business, and partly because they fail to understand the very real and demonstrable relationship between customer retention and profitability.

The effect of long-term relationships with customers can be explained by the following reasons:

The effect of customer retention on profits

- Acquiring a new customer costs more than retaining an existing one.

- Normally 80 per cent of the profits are derived from 20 per cent of the clients (according to the Pareto Principle) — it thus makes sense to concentrate on those clients that produce profits; in other words, the existing clients.

- Regular customers tend to place frequent and consistent orders, thereby decreasing the costs of servicing those customers.

- Efforts to retain customers make it difficult for competitors to enter the market or to increase their share of the market.

- Improved customer retention can lead to an increased level of employee satisfaction, which leads to increased employee retention, and which feeds back into an even greater customer longevity.

- Long-time customers tend to be less price sensitive, permitting the charging of higher prices — they will not move for the extra 5 per cent difference in banking charges, for example.

- Long-time customers are likely to provide free word-of-mouth advertising and referrals.

Customer retention can be improved upon if the organisation focuses on customer migration.

2.5.3 Customer Migration

Organisations should not only focus on customer retention as such, but they need to investigate customer migration before it leads to defection.[25] Upward migration means that customers spend more, while downward migration refers to customers spending less and less. Managing migration — from the satisfied customers who spend more to the downward migrators who spend less — is crucial in customer-retention strategies.

Many more customers change their spending behaviour than defect. So the spending behaviour typically accounts for larger changes in value.

Migration and defection at a bank[26]

A bank found the following interesting facts when it investigated migration and defection:

- About 5 per cent of its cheque account customers defected annually, taking with them 10 per cent of the bank's cheque accounts and 3 per cent of its total balances;

- but every year, the 35 per cent of customers who reduced their balances (i.e. downward migration) significantly cost the bank 24 per cent of its total balances;

- while the 35 per cent who increased their balances (i.e. upward migration) raised its total balances by 25 per cent.

Managing migration not only gives companies an early chance to stem the downward course before their customers defect entirely, but also helps them influence upward migration earlier. One should also keep in mind that a broad measure of satisfaction can tell a company how likely customers are to defect, but satisfaction alone does not tell an organisation what makes customers loyal — the product, or the difficulty of finding a replacement, for example, can also be factors. Nor does gauging satisfaction levels tell an organisation how susceptible its customers are to changing their spending patterns. Understanding the other drivers of loyalty is crucial to having an influence on migration.

Normally, customers are loyal because they are emotionally attached to the supplier, and have rationally chosen it as the best option. Downward migrators have several reasons for spending less: their lifestyle has changed, so they have developed new needs that the organisation is not meeting; they continually reassess their options and have found a better one; or they are actively dissatisfied, often because of a single bad experience (e.g. with a rude salesperson).

Organisations often make little effort to meet their customers' changing needs, which might include new financial or insurance products for ageing customers, and new travel arrangements made necessary by updated corporate travel policies. Changing needs are not uncontrollable — they can be addressed, and these new needs form a relevant part of the overall loyalty opportunity.

The case for increasing customer retention is captured in the concept of customer lifetime value.[27] Organisations can use their customer database to determine how profitable existing customers are before expensive efforts are made to retain them.

2.5.4 Customer Lifetime Value

The old concept of lifetime value (CLV) has been revived by CRM and has become one of its key tenets of CRM in that it recognises the value of customers over their purchasing lifetimes.[28] In recognising lifetime value, CRM seeks to bond progressively more firmly with customers.

Customer lifetime value can be defined as *the present value of the stream of future profits expected over the customer's lifetime purchases*. CLV is estimated by using past behaviours to forecast the future purchases, gross margin from these purchases, and costs associated with servicing the customer.[29] Costs associated with a customer include the cost of advertising and promotions used to acquire the customer and the cost of goods returned. Other costs could include such factors as the profit earned on referrals made by a customer, the monetary value of collaborative assistance from the customer in designing new products or services, the benefit of the customer's own reputation among other current and potential customers, and so on. The figure you could come up with if you were able to factor in all these variables is the customer's lifetime value.

The assessment of CLV is based on the assumption that the customer's future purchase behaviours will be the same as they have been in the past. Sophisticated statistical methods are typically used to estimate the future contributions from past purchases. For example, these methods might consider how recent purchases have been made. The expected CLV of a customer at a grocery store who purchased R2 000 on one visit, for instance, is probably less than the CLV of a customer who has been purchasing R500 of merchandise every month for the last six months.

CLV may stand out as fairly clear-cut for consumers, although one has to consider that certain goods such as nappies and baby food, for example, are only of interest during a limited period in a family's lifetime.

Customers have different values to a business, and they need different things from the business. What do the customers want and what is the customer worth? The value of a customer relative to other customers allows the business to prioritise its efforts, allocating more resources to ensuring that the more valuable customers remain loyal and grow in value.[30] And catering to what a specific customer needs is the basis for creating a relationship and winning customers' loyalty. It is therefore necessary to rank customers by their value and to differentiate them by their needs.

There is one other critical element of the customer's lifetime value: the customer's growth potential or strategic value. Strategic value is *the additional value a customer could yield if you had a strategy to get it*.[31]

A customer's growth potential or strategic value

A banking customer has both a cheque and a savings account. Every month the customer provides a certain profit to the bank, and the net present value of this continuing profit stream represents the customer's actual value to the bank. But the home mortgage that same customer has at a competitive bank represents strategic value — potential value that the first bank could realise if it had a proactive strategy to obtain it.

Knowing both actual and strategic value allows an organisation to calculate its 'share of wallet' (i.e. the percentage of the customer's purchases made from the organisation) with these customers. Remember, you cannot calculate this precisely. Instead, you create a financial model for it, try to get a better and better handle on it, and in the end, settle for a good-enough substitute variable. A simple way of calculating the lifetime value of an average supermarket customer can be done as follows:

CLV of a supermarket customer

The customer's expenditure per week	R800
Thus she spends per month	R3 200
She spends per year	R38 400
Assume she remains loyal for 20 years	x 20
Then her lifetime value is	R768 000

However, as you can see, no costs have yet been calculated, such as advertising, so the actual lifetime value would be less.

Kotler proposes the following more sophisticated way of estimating CLV:[32]

When an organisation has determined the CLV of its customers, it should have a well-informed financial view of its customer base. In particular, it will know that a relatively small number of customers account for the majority of the profits. A retailer, for example, could group its customers into a commonly used segmentation scheme that divides customers into four segments, as illustrated in figure 2.1.

Calculating CLV

A company could analyse its new-customer acquisition cost as follows:

Cost of an average sales call (including salary, commission, benefits and expenses)	$300
Average number of sales calls to convert an average prospect into a customer	x 4
Cost of attracting a new customer	$1 200

This is an underestimate, because we are omitting the cost of advertising and promotion, plus the fact that only a fraction of all potential customers end up being converted into actual customers.

Now suppose the company estimates average customer lifetime value as follows:

Annual customer revenue	$5 000
Average number of loyal years	x 2
Company profit margin	0.1
Customer lifetime value	$1 000

This company is spending more to attract new customers than they are worth. Unless the company can sign up customers with fewer sales calls, spend less per sales call, stimulate higher new-customer annual spending, retain customers longer, or sell them higher-profit products, it is headed for bankruptcy.

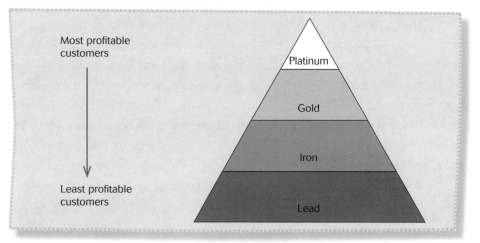

Most profitable customers

Least profitable customers

Platinum

Gold

Iron

Lead

Figure 2.1 The Customer Pyramid[33]

Let us look at each of these segments:

- **Platinum segment:** This segment is composed of the customers with the top 25 per cent CLVs. Typically, these are the most loyal customers who are not overly concerned about price, and place more value on customer service.
- **Gold segment:** The next 25 per cent of customers have a lower CLV than platinum customers because they are more price sensitive. Even though they buy a significant number of products, they are not as loyal as platinum customers and probably patronise competitors as well.
- **Iron segment:** These customers do not deserve much special attention due to their modest CLV.
- **Lead segment:** These customers are in the lowest segment, and often demand much attention but do not buy much. They, in fact, cost the organisation money.

In the same way as the customer pyramid, segmentation schemes can be drawn up for other types of companies, such as airlines. However, the pyramid will be quite different. Some schemes break customers into ten deciles according to their CLV, rather than the quartiles illustrated above. In this case, the 10 per cent of the customers with the highest LTV would be in the top segment. (In chapter 8 targeting customers based on their profitability will be discussed.)

When segments or segmentation schemes are designed, a good starting point is to investigate the stages of relationship development.

2.6 Stages of Relationship Development

Customers display a different economic sense. Once a customer has been acquired, the relationship with the company can develop in two fundamentally different directions, depending on the level of customer satisfaction. On the one hand, if the company is able to keep a customer lastingly satisfied, ideally the customer may turn into an 'enthusiast' of the company. This means the customer becomes more and more loyal, making significant use of the entire range of company services, while not considering competitive offers. On the other hand, in the case of a customer who becomes dissatisfied, it is possible that the customer may even turn into a 'terrorist' with regard to the company, not only by causing the organisation extra costs, but also by dissuading other current or potential customers from dealing with the organisation.[34]

The well-known relationship marketing (or CRM) ladder of loyalty identifies five stages of relationship development, and these also represent the different stages of relationship development, or customer bonding, in order to achieve loyalty. This ladder of loyalty is illustrated in figure 2.2.[35]

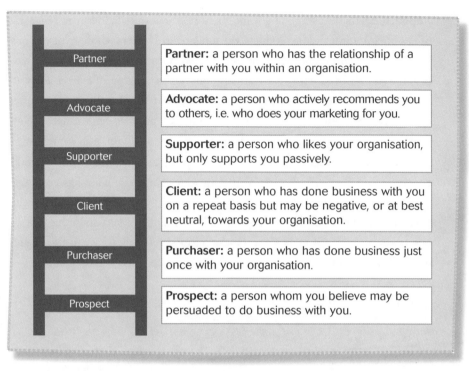

Partner: a person who has the relationship of a partner with you within an organisation.

Advocate: a person who actively recommends you to others, i.e. who does your marketing for you.

Supporter: a person who likes your organisation, but only supports you passively.

Client: a person who has done business with you on a repeat basis but may be negative, or at best neutral, towards your organisation.

Purchaser: a person who has done business just once with your organisation.

Prospect: a person whom you believe may be persuaded to do business with you.

Figure 2.2 The Relationship Marketing Ladder of Loyalty

Prospects: The first task is to identify *prospects* who offer interesting potential and may want to do business with you. Prospects usually have limited awareness of an organisation and its relevance, but are unlikely to become purchasers until awareness increases. Thus, elevating levels of company or product/service awareness may be an important issue for shifting customers from prospects to purchasers. These prospects then need to be moved up to the first rung to become a *purchaser*.

Purchaser: During the *purchaser* phase, potential consumers have begun to explore the extent to which your company is relevant to them, perhaps with initial trial purchases. Based on their satisfaction with this experience, they will wish to assess the potential to establish a more significant flow of business to your company. Needless to say, excellent service and follow-up interaction are important in moving these customers to the next rung on the ladder.

Client: The company should now try to turn the new purchaser into a *client* who purchases regularly. If clients are satisfied with all their contact with the company, they may become more significant. Even small mistakes or problems can create the dissatisfaction that can erode the trust relationship that is beginning to be forged in this stage.

Supporter: The next stage of advancement up the loyalty ladder is the *supporter* of the organisation and its products, the longer-term buyers whose trust you now have. These consumers, who are satisfied with their initial experience, have begun to do business with your company, but not as a matter of course. They are likely to continue to do business with their current supplier, but are interested enough in your offer that they consider your company an appropriate second source in the event that their main supplier fails to satisfy them in some way.

Advocate: The advocate on the next rung provides powerful word-of-mouth endorsement of an organisation. With advocates, your company has customers who are so committed to your organisation that only a major violation of trust would erode this goodwill. You have virtually their entire attention in this product or service category. An advocate will make business referrals; they will also be *good complainers*, inviting you to improve without being negative in their guidance.

Bonding at advocate level[36]

Saturn, a division of General Motors, has succeeded in bonding with customers at this level. Saturn hosted an event to invite owners to come to the factory where their cars were built. Thousands enjoyed a rain-soaked weekend in a muddy field, without complaint. When a Saturn owner's T-shirt invites people to ask him/her about his/her happy ownership experience, Saturn can claim customer bonding that goes far beyond the relationship most people have with many other car companies.

Partner: In an organisation-to-organisation context, advocates may ultimately develop into *partners* who are closely linked in trusting and mutually sharing relationships with their suppliers. Satisfied with the period during which your company has been catering to their needs, the consumers, in this stage, include your company as a major supplier for their needs. You now have their trust.

2.7 Summary

CRM focuses on improving learning relationships with customers. These learning relationships are based on obtaining information by interacting with customers. An organisation cannot, however, focus on all relationships, since some are simply not appropriate, and thus do not justify the time and money that need to be invested to maintain them. In order to build and improve relationships, marketers need to take into account the essential requirements for a relationship, namely *trust, commitment, shared goals* and *mutual benefits*, as, without these, the relationship would not be successful. The main reason why a marketer wants to build these relationships is to create customer loyalty, which means that customer retention, customer migration and the lifetime value of customers are important factors to be considered. Once the profitability of customers has been established, different strategies of loyalty can be put in place, depending on the nature of the customer's profitability and loyalty. (These strategies will be dealt with in chapter 8.)

Discussion Questions

1. How can a learning relationship be built between a customer and his/her bank where almost all his/her accounts are kept?

2. Why are some relationships unrealistic? Illustrate your answer with practical examples.

3. Explain, with the aid of practical examples, the essential ingredients of a relationship, highlighting how these ingredients should be applied by a bank.

4. Explain and illustrate why a marketer should take into account customer retention and customer migration in order to develop customer loyalty.

5. An organisation wishing to determine the profitability of its customers has requested that you explain the lifetime value of customers to it, and to illustrate how this value can be determined and applied by the organisation. Explain how you would approach this request.

6. What are the segments of the customer pyramid?

7. How should a firm of attorneys use the stages of relationship development to attract and keep more clients?

Mini Case Study

Jenny Brown is on her third business trip this month. She takes a taxi from Boston's Logan Airport to the Ritz-Carlton, her favourite hotel. As the doorman opens the car door for her, he greets her, 'Welcome back to the Ritz-Carlton, Mrs Brown'. When she goes to the registration desk, the receptionist also greets her, gives her the room key and asks if she would like to have her stay charged to her American Express card, as usual. Then she goes to her room and finds just what she prefers – a room with a view of the Boston Commons, a single queen-sized bed, an extra pillow and blanket, a fax machine connected to her telephone, and a basket with her favourite fruit and snacks.

Question

Can you identify the important factors in building relationships with customers that the Ritz-Carlton has implemented in terms of the following?

(a) learning relationship

(b) customer database

(c) customer retention

(d) lifetime value

(e) managing customer loyalty.

References

1   Gibbons, C. 1999. *The Future of Customer Relationship* Management, 1, October, p. 2.

2   Peppers, D & Rogers, M. 1999. *Enterprise One to One.* New York: Currency Doubleday, p. 15.

3   Gilmore, JH & Pine, BJ. 2000. *Markets of One.* Boston: Harvard Business School Publishing, p. 54.

4   Levy, M & Weitz, BA. 2004. *Retailing Management* (5th ed.). New York: McGraw-Hill, pp. 338–39.

5   Peppers, D, Rogers, M & Dorf, B. 1999. *One to One Fieldbook.* New York: Currency Doubleday, pp. 96–99.

6   *Ibid.*, p. 98.

7   *Ibid.*, p. 103.

8   Peck, H, Payne, A, Christopher, M & Clark, M. 1999. *Relationship Marketing Strategy and Implementation.* Oxford: Butterworth-Heinemann, p. 46.

9   Gilmore & Pine, *op. cit.*, p. 58.

10   Egan, J. 2001. *Relationship Marketing.* London: Pearson Education, pp. 42–43.

11   *Ibid.*, p. 91.

12   Morgan, RM & Hunt, SD. 1994. The commitment-trust theory of relationship marketing. *Journal of Marketing*, 58, pp. 20–38.

13   Morris, DS, Barnes, BR & Lynch, JE. 1999. Relationship marketing needs total quality management. *Total Quality Management*, 10 (4&5), July, p. S660.

14   *Ibid.*

15   Abramson, NR & Ai, JX. 1998/9. Practising relationship marketing. *Management International Review*, 38, special issue, pp. 113–20.

16   Egan, *op. cit.*, p. 15.

17   Abramson & Ai, *op. cit.*, p. 118.

18   Levy & Weitz, *op. cit.*, p. 336.

19   Egan, *op. cit.*, p. 37.

20   Brink, A, Strydom, JW, Cant, MC & Machado, R. 2001. *Relationship Marketing.* Pretoria: Unisa Centre for Business Management.

21   Hey, A. 1997. *Marketplace*, 26 May, p. 10.

3

22 Based on Payne, A. 2000. Customer retention in Cranfield School of Management. *Marketing Management: A Relationship Marketing Perspective.* New York: St Martin's Press, pp. 110–22.

23 Brink *et al.*, *op. cit.*, pp. 3–5.

24 *Ibid.*, p. 4.

25 Coyles, S & Gokey, TC. 2002. Customer retention is not enough. *McKinsey Quarterly*, 2, pp. 82–83.

26 *Ibid.*, p. 83.

27 Kotler, A. 2003. *Marketing Management.* Upper Saddle River: Pearson Education, p. 75.

28 Gummesson, E. 2002. *Total Relationship Marketing.* Oxford: Butterworth-Heinemann, p. 234.

29 Levy & Weitz, *op. cit.*, p. 346.

30 Peppers *et al.*, *op. cit.*, pp. 56–58.

31 *Ibid.*, p. 58.

32 Kotler, *op. cit.*, pp. 75–76.

33 Levy & Weitz, *op. cit.*, p. 346.

34 Osarenkhoe A & Bennani, A. 2007. An exploratory study of implementation of customer relationship management strategy. *Business Process Management Journal*, 13 (1), p. 146.

35 Peck *et al.*, *op. cit.*, pp. 45–46; Gordon, IH. 1998. *Relationship Marketing.* Toronto: John Wiley, pp. 100–3.

36 Gordon, *op. cit.*, p. 103.

C H A P T E R

3

Service Issues in RM and CRM

Learning Outcomes

After studying this chapter, you should be able to:

- explain the nature of customer service by highlighting its meaning and its role in building customer relationships

- discuss customer expectations

- explain and illustrate the factors involved in service quality

- demonstrate the links between relationships, quality service and customer loyalty

- explain ways of measuring customer satisfaction

- discuss the factors involved in moments of truth or service encounters

- identify and explain the various factors that shape servicescapes

- explain the impact of service failure and how service recovery can lead to customer satisfaction

- explain the key success factors of service management

- explain the relevance, for keeping customers, of the cash value or lifetime value of each customer

- identify some of the elements of great service

- discuss the management of the service culture within an organisation.

3.1 Introduction

In South Africa, poor customer service is particularly prevalent in the food and retail industry. This is according to the findings in a national customer satisfaction study by research company, React Surveys.[1] It was found that many consumers had a lot more disposable income and were spending money 'without being too fussy' about the service. It is therefore easier to be rude to a customer because there are 100 more behind him or her! The survey also found that most customers returned to the stores and restaurants that provided bad service because of value for money and convenience. Furthermore, shoppers believe it does not pay to complain about bad service in restaurants and retail stores.

Customer service, an integral part of CRM, can be used to differentiate a company from its competitors, yet we know there are not that many companies that are recognised as giving good service. Think of South African companies that could be considered 'excellent' in terms of service. Woolworths is one company that often comes to mind in this regard. It has certainly managed to differentiate itself in terms of product and service quality, and is reaping the rewards of this through premier pricing. Yet even Woolworths went through a difficult period when it had to refocus its efforts in terms of the strategic direction of its services and quality to maintain its performance in the marketplace. Therefore, even though an organisation knows what it wants to achieve in terms of service and quality, achieving those objectives is clearly more difficult than it seems, as evidenced by the few companies that can really be considered as giving excellent service.

High-quality customer service is the key to improving relationships with customers, and an enhanced relationship with one's customers can ultimately lead to greater customer retention, customer loyalty and, more importantly, profitability.[2] Customer satisfaction is hard to win and easy to lose; if customers are not satisfied, they will simply move on to other companies.

In today's highly competitive environment, companies must pay attention to fulfilling the needs of each customer quickly and accurately. If an organisation can position itself favourably within a particular marketplace, relative to competitors, it has created a competitive advantage; indeed, stronger relationships with customers result in a number of competitive advantages.

In this chapter, the nature of customer service will be described first, followed by service quality and customer expectations of service quality. Other factors to be discussed are the links between relationships, quality service and loyalty; the moments of truth (or service encounters); and servicescapes. Various other important factors in creating a service culture within and organisation will also be dealt with.

3.2 The Nature of Customer Service

Let us first see what customer service means.

3.2.1 What Is Customer Service?

Customer service is *the provision of service to customers before, during and after a purchase*. Essentially, customer service is any back-up service that the company provides to customers to maintain their loyalty and to secure a sale. In relationship marketing, customer service must be seen in the context of the supply/marketing channel. This view of the supply/marketing channel suggests that customer service should be seen not just in the context of the company and its relationship with its customers, but also in its downstream relationship with its ultimate customers, as well as its upstream relationship with suppliers.

The actual distribution of goods may represent much of the customer service element for a manufacturer supplying branded goods to distribution companies. Similarly, the ability of suppliers to be able to meet promised delivery schedules is the most frequently mentioned aspect of service referred to by buyers.

While to a distributor, delivery schedules may be the most important, other service elements may be relevant to the final consumer. It is for this reason that warranties, unconditional service guarantees, intelligible (i.e. clear and simple) instruction books and free phone-in advice centres become critical to customer service.

It must be kept in mind that it is not the actual service that is of importance, but rather the *perceptions* that a customer has of the service. Therefore one should always try to see the overall service from the customer's point of view.

Customers have expectations of how they think a service will be provided. These expectations are based on their past experiences, what they have heard from their friends and family, and what they have seen in the media, either in advertisements or news reports.

Service and Customer Service are becoming more important to consumers and organisations, as they impact on the way in which relationships are built. Let us consider the following arguments in this regard:

- **Changing customer expectations:** In almost every market, the customer is now more demanding, knowledgeable and sophisticated than he/she was, say, thirty years ago. Customers have higher expectations and more choices than ever before. This means that marketers have to listen more closely to customers than ever before. They also have to anticipate needs, to solve problems before they start, to provide service that impresses customers, and to offer responses to mistakes that more than make up for the original error. Competitors have not only been meeting these rising customer expectations, but shaping them with yet higher standards of performance and value. And so the cycle repeats itself, with customers asking for more and getting it. So there is no reason why customers should buy one organisation's offerings unless it is in some way better at serving the customers' needs than those offered by competing organisations.

- **The increased importance of customer service:** With changing customer expectations, competitors are seeing customer service as an important competitive weapon by means of which to distinguish their product(s) from competitors' offerings, thereby successfully differentiating their sales efforts.

- **The need for a relationship strategy:** To ensure a customer service strategy that is formulated, implemented and controlled, and that will create attractive value for customers, it is necessary to establish this strategy as having a central role and not one that is only a sub-component of the elements of the marketing mix.

In the next section, key issues in building relationships through customer service will be detailed.

3.2.2 Customer Service in Building Relationships[3]

Organisations that embrace the marketing concept seek ways to build a profitable long-term relationship with each customer. Even the most innovative organisation faces competition sooner or later. And trying to get new customers by taking them away from a competitor is usually more costly than retaining current customers by really satisfying their needs; satisfied customers buy again and again. This makes the customer's buying job easier, and it also increases the selling organisation's profits. Thus, in an organisation that has adopted the marketing concept with its focus on customer orientation, everyone focuses on customer satisfaction in order to offer superior customer value. That helps to attract customers in the first place — and keeps them satisfied after they buy. Because customers are satisfied, they want to purchase from the organisation again. The relationship with customers is profitable, so the organisation is encouraged to find better ways to offer superior customer value. In other words, when a firm adopts the marketing concept, it wins and so do its customers.

Most successful marketers understand that key issues in developing competitive advantage include building long-term relationships, and central to these relationships are maintaining customer satisfaction and creating customer value.

Customer satisfaction

A marketer who adopts the marketing concept sees customer satisfaction as the path to profits. To ensure survival and success, organisations therefore have to satisfy their customers.

Customer satisfaction is the customer's feeling that a product has met or exceeded his/her expectations. Organisations that have a reputation for delivering high levels of customer satisfaction do things differently from their competitors. Top management is obsessed with customer satisfaction, and employees throughout the organisation understand the link between their job and satisfied customers. The culture of the organisation is to focus on satisfying customers rather than on selling products. Such companies do not pursue one-time transactions; they cultivate relationships.

For an organisation to be focused on customer satisfaction in order to build relationships with customers, employees' attitudes and actions must be customer oriented. An employee may be the only contact a particular customer has with the business. In that customer's eyes, the employee is the business. Any person, department or division that is not customer oriented weakens the positive image of the entire business. For example, a potential customer who is greeted discourteously may well assume that the employee's attitude represents the whole organisation. Leading marketers recognise the role of employee training in customer service to build customer relationships. Consider, for example, how all new employees at Disneyland and Walt Disney World must attend Disney University, a special training programme for Disney employees. Similarly, McDonald's has its own Hamburger University.

Customer value

Building relationships with customers requires that all the employees in an organisation work together to provide customer value before and after each purchase. The long-term relationship with the customer is threatened unless everyone works together to make things right for the customer when he/she has a complaint about service or quality. Any time the customer value is reduced — because the benefits to the customer decrease or the costs increase — the relationship is weakened.

Customer value is the ratio of benefits to the sacrifice (by the customer) necessary to obtain those benefits.

Lexus: Customer driven

In the fiercely competitive motorcar industry, for example, Lexus adopted a customer-driven approach, with particular emphasis on service. Lexus stresses product quality with a standard of zero defects in manufacturing. The service quality goal is to treat each customer as one would treat a guest in one's home, to pursue the perfect person-to-person relationship and to strive to improve continually. This pursuit has enabled Lexus to establish a clear quality image and capture a significant share of the luxury car market.

Customer value is not simply a matter of high quality; thus a high-quality product that is available only at a high price will not be perceived as good value, nor will bare-bones service or low-quality goods selling for a low price. Instead, customers value goods and services of the quality they expect that are sold at prices they are willing to pay. Value can be used to sell a top-of-the-range Mercedes-Benz as well as a R30 KFC dinner!

To offer customer value, marketers need to consider the following broad guidelines:

- The bare minimum requirement is to offer products that do what they're meant to do; consumers lose patience with shoddy merchandise that doesn't work properly.
- Give customers more than they expect by delivering the best customer experience in the market you serve. The customer experience is the sum total of the interactions that a customer has with a company's product, people and processes; in other words, give customers more than they expect.
- Give customers adequate information. Today's sophisticated consumer wants informative advertising and knowledgeable salespeople.
- Offer organisation-wide commitment in service and after-sales support.

Southwest Airlines offers value

People fly Southwest Airlines because it offers superior value. Although passengers do not get assigned seats or meals when they use the airline, its service is reliable and friendly and costs less than most other airlines. All employees are involved in the effort to satisfy customers. Pilots help at the boarding gate if their help is needed and ticket agents help move luggage. One reservation agent flew from Dallas to Tulsa with a frail elderly woman whose son was afraid she could not handle the change of planes by herself on her way to St Louis!

So, the higher the perceived benefit of a product or service, the higher the customer value and the greater the chance that the customer will choose and keep choosing the product or service in future.

In the next section, customer expectations of service quality will be discussed.

3.3 Customer Expectations

Central to the effective management of customer service within any organisation has to be the issue of service quality performance. Service quality is *the ability of the organisation to meet or exceed customer expectations.* In this context, customer expectations may be seen as the desires or wants of consumers; in other words, what consumers feel a service provider should offer rather than what it does offer. Thus, service quality is measured in terms of the extent to which an organisation's performance is perceived by customers as meeting or exceeding expectations. It is, therefore, the customers' *perceptions* of performance that count, rather than the reality of performance. Indeed, it can be argued that as far as service quality is concerned, 'perceptions are reality'.[4]

The organisation should know how the customers compare its service in terms of service expected and actual service received (or experienced).

3.3.1 Service Expected vs Service Received

Customers' expectations are based on their knowledge of and experiences with a particular organisation and its competitors. For example, customers expect a supermarket to have parking facilities. Marketers can also provide unexpected services to increase their competitive advantage and to outsmart competitors.

Unexpected service

- A hotel sends customers home in a taxi because they have had too much to drink.

- A gift store keeps track of important customers' celebration dates and suggests appropriate gifts.

- An airline remembers your seat preference (aisle or window).

Delivering quality service means conforming to customer expectations on a consistent basis. Service quality is thus a measure of how well the level of service delivered matches customer expectations. In line with this thinking, Grönroos[5] developed a model in which he contends that consumers compare the service they expect with perceptions of the service they receive in evaluating service quality. As shown in the row of four boxes at the bottom of figure 3.1, four quality outcomes are possible.

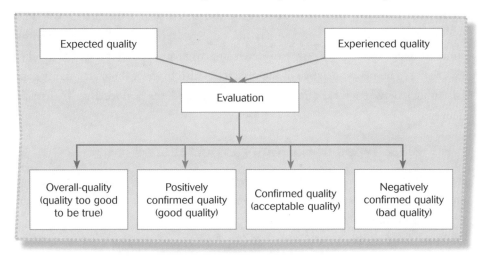

Figure 3.1 Possible Quality Outcomes

During and after the service, the customer will start to evaluate it. This evaluation is based on the expected quality that the customer had prior to the service and the quality that the customer perceives during the service, which will lead to different quality options, as shown in figure 3.1. For example, if the customer has very high expectations of the service and the service is average, the quality will be negatively confirmed. However, if the customer has very low expectations of the service and the service is average, the quality will be positively confirmed.

There is usually a big difference between what the expected quality is and the quality that is actually delivered. In evaluating quality, the customer has four possible quality experiences, namely:

- **Excessive quality:** This is a situation where even the customer realises that more is delivered than is economically justified.
- **Positively confirmed quality** is a situation where a little more is delivered than the customer expected. This situation is called 'customer delight' and makes the customer feel positive about continuing the relationship with the organisation. This also leads to good word-of-mouth communication about the organisation, and its products and services.
- **Confirmed quality** is the minimum quality that the customer will accept, but which does not necessarily make the customer feel that he or she must continue the relationship with the organisation.

🔻 **Negatively confirmed quality** is a bad quality experience by the customer, which will result in the customer breaking the relationship with the organisation and spreading negative word-of-mouth communications about it.

Quality is obviously situation- or organisation-specific, and the benchmark that may represent high quality today may not be perceived as such in a few months' time. Market research is needed to determine what precisely represents a quality experience. The main objective of the research is also to see if there are quality gaps (shortfalls) between what the customer expects and the service that is actually delivered.

3.3.2 Types of Customer Expectations[6]

Expectations serve as benchmarks against which present and future service encounters are compared. It is useful to distinguish the following three different types of expectation.

🔻 **Predicted service:** This reflects the level of service customers believe is likely to occur. For example, bank customers tend to conduct their banking business at the same bank over time. They become accustomed to dealing with the personnel at the bank and begin to anticipate certain performance levels. It is generally agreed that customer satisfaction evaluations are developed by comparing predicted service to perceived service received.

🔻 **Desired service:** This is an ideal expectation that reflects what customers actually want compared with predicted service, which is what is likely to occur. Hence, in most instances, desired service reflects a higher expectation than predicted service. For example, a bank customer's desired service is that he/she not only receives his/her predicted service, but that the tellers call him/her by his/her first name and enthusiastically greet him/her as he/she enters the bank. Comparing desired service expectations to perceived service received results in a measure of perceived service superiority.

🔻 **Adequate service:** This reflects a minimum tolerable expectation and reflects the level of service the customer is willing to accept. Adequate service is based on experiences or norms that develop over time. For example, most adult consumers have dined at hundreds of restaurants. Through these experiences, norms develop that consumers expect to occur. Hence, one factor that influences adequate service is predicted service. Encounters that fall below expected norms fall below adequate service expectations. Comparing adequate service with perceived service produces a measure of perceived service adequacy.

3.3.3 Zone of Tolerance

The difference between the desired service level and the adequate service level can be called the zone of tolerance, i.e. *the extent to which customers recognise and are willing to accept variation in service delivery from one location to the next and even with the same provider from one day to the next*. Consumers who accept this variation develop a zone of tolerance. The zone of tolerance expands and contracts across customers and within the same customer depending on the service and the conditions under which the service is provided. Other factors, such as price, may influence the zone of tolerance, e.g. as the price increases, the customer's zone of tolerance decreases as desired service needs begin to dominate, and the customer becomes less forgiving of sloppy service.

3.3.4 Factors Influencing Service Expectations

Desired service expectations are developed as a result of the following different sources:

- **Enduring service intensifiers:** These intensifiers are personal factors that are stable over time and that increase a customer's sensitivity to how the service should best be provided. For example, the customer's personal service philosophies or personal view of the meaning of service and the way in which service providers should conduct themselves will heighten his or her sensitivities. These customers hold their own views regarding exactly how service should be provided; they want to be treated in the way they believe they should be treated.

- **Personal needs:** The customer's own personal needs influence desired service expectations. Some customers are needier than others. Some customers are very particular about where they are seated in a restaurant, while others are happy to sit nearly anywhere. In a hotel, some customers are very interested in the hotel's amenities, such as the pool, sauna, dining room and other forms of available entertainment, while others are simply looking for a clean room. Customers have a variety of needs, and no two are alike in every way, thus the organisation is particularly challenged in providing a service.

- **Explicit service promises:** These encompass the organisation's advertising, personal selling, contracts and other forms of communication. The more ambiguous the service, the more customers rely on the organisation's advertising when forming expectations. For example, if a hotel stresses modern and clean rooms, customers expect the rooms to be exactly the way they were pictured in the advertisement.

- **Implicit service promises:** These promises also influence desired service and predicted service. As the price increases, customers expect the organisation to deliver higher-quality services. For example, customers would probably have higher expectations of service at a higher-priced hair salon than they would of a cheaper barber's shop. The nicer the furnishings of the organisation, the higher customer expectations become.

- **Word-of-mouth communications:** Customers tend to rely more on personal sources of information than on non-personal ones when choosing a service provider. Customers view word-of-mouth information as unbiased information from someone who has been through the service experience. Sources of word-of-mouth information range from friends, family or consultants to product review publications such as the magazine *Getaway*.

- **Past experience:** Service evaluations are often based on a comparison of the current service encounter to other encounters with the same provides, other providers in the industry and other providers in another industry. In a college, for example, students' desired and predicted service expectations of lecturers are likely to be based on past experience in other classes with the same lecturer and on other classes with other lecturers.

In the next section, service quality will be looked at in greater detail.

3.4   Service Quality

In section 3.3, above, the concept of quality was introduced in a service context. Service quality comes about through a focused evaluation reflecting the customer's perception of specific dimensions of service.

> ### Definition of service quality
>
> Service quality can be defined as *the ability of an organisation to determine customer expectations correctly and to deliver the service at a quality level that will at least equal these customer expectations.*[7]

Service quality, as perceived by the customer, is one of the components that would influence the satisfaction of the customer. Although promises of quality may attract customers, marketers (especially service providers), believe that the delivery of quality is essential in building and maintaining customer relationships.[8] Delivering on promises is the essence of mutually satisfying relationships. Service quality refers to the consistency with which customers' expectations are met and the general superiority of the service relative to that of the competition. Accordingly, this initiative includes any practices focused on identifying what services and service attributes customers want and providing them to the customers' satisfaction and at a level superior to the competition. This includes efforts to raise standards and improve service performance, listening to customers' preferences and ensuring that customers' requirements are met. Providing friendly, professional, courteous service that is consistent, fair and reliable is one of the best ways to establish and maintain customer relationships. This is exemplified by making on-time deliveries, supplying a wide range of goods and service, having a knowledgeable staff and providing technical competence. Service quality includes listening to customers — knowing the market and understanding customers' needs. Naturally, consistently meeting customers' expectations includes responses focusing on providing high quality goods and services.

Let us consider the different views as to what constitutes service quality from the customer's point of view.

3.4.1 Evaluating Service Quality

One way of evaluating service quality is by considering two factors:[9]

- the technical quality of the outcome of service delivery; and
- the functional quality of the service delivery process.

If a service has a specific outcome, such as winning a court case, then a customer can make a judgement on the effectiveness of the service on the basis of the particular outcome (i.e. winning or losing the case). If the service is complex, however, and an outcome is not clear, it may be hard to judge a service on the outcome. The customer could then rely on *how* the service was done in order to determine quality — in other words, the service is judged by looking at the process (the way it was done).

Judging service quality: Architects

The services provided by architects are very complex, and the outcome is not always easy to judge. Understanding the process and outcome quality can be important for the success of an architect. If two architects both have good technical skills and certificates, but one has very good interpersonal skills, then the process dimensions such as the ability to solve problems, to empathise and to meet deadlines, as well as being courteous, could lead to an advantage for one over the other.

3.4.2 Dimensions Used for Evaluating Service Quality

As a result of exploratory and quantitative studies, researchers have identified five dimensions that consumers use in order to assess service quality. These dimensions apply across a wide range of industries, but it would be important for a marketer to establish how critical each of the dimensions is to a specific target group. This would help guide the marketer as to which dimension to focus on in that specific segment. The five dimensions are as follows:

Reliability

Reliability refers to the ability to perform the promised service dependably and accurately, and focuses on delivering on promises made by the organisation. Customers expect companies to keep their promises, because, if the organisation does not deliver the core service that customers think they are buying, it will be seen as failing them. Think of other companies that you tend to use — more likely than not, they are the ones that are consistent and reliable. Loyalty, as noted in the previous sections, cannot be earned without consistent and reliable service.

Responsiveness

This is the willingness to help customers and provide prompt service. Responsiveness implies that the needs of the customer are met in a timely manner, and that the organisation is flexible enough to customise a service to the specific customer's needs. It is critical to understand the customer's expectations in terms of time (speed) in order to understand what must be done to be seen as responsive.

Assurance

Assurance refers to the knowledge and courtesy of employees, and their ability to convey trust and confidence. This is important in those services that are perceived as high risk, or where the customer is not sure about how to evaluate outcomes. Examples of these would be banking, insurance and medical services.

Empathy

The caring, individualised attention a firm gives its customers is known as empathy. This involves confirming for the customer that his/her unique needs and requirements will be met. Many smaller companies can compete with big companies through convincing the customer that they understand him/her better, unlike the cold, formal, by-the-numbers approach of many larger companies. Being perceived as a specialist in a certain field could also help a company to be seen as being able to meet specialised needs of customers better than others can.

Tangibles

Tangibles include the appearance of physical facilities (offices, showrooms, consulting rooms), equipment, staff and communication materials; in other words, anything physical that indicates to customers the quality of the service that they will receive. This is especially important for a new customer, who looks for cues as to the level of service he/she should expect. Table 3.1 shows how these five dimensions of service quality can be used to judge the quality of a variety of services.

Table 3.1 Service Quality Dimensions for Selected Industries[10]

Industry	Reliability	Responsive-ness	Assurance	Empathy	Tangibles
Car repair (consumer)	Problem fixed the first time and car ready when promised	Accessible; no waiting; responds to requests	Knowledge-able mechanics	Acknow-ledges customer by name; remembers previous problems and preferences	Repair facility; waiting area; uniforms; equipment
Airline (consumer)	Flights to promised destinations depart and arrive on schedule	Prompt and speedy system for ticketing, in-flight, baggage handling	Trusted name; good safety record; competent employees	Understanding of special individual needs; anticipates customer needs	Aircraft; ticketing counters; baggage area; uniforms
Medical care	Appointments are kept on schedule; diagnoses prove to be accurate	Accessible; no waiting; willingness to listen	Knowledge; skills; credentials; reputation	Acknow-ledges patient as a person; remembers previous problems; good listening; patience	Waiting room; examination room; equipment; written materials

In the next sections, the link between quality service and loyalty is investigated.

3.5 Quality Service and Customer Loyalty[11]

In chapters 1 and 2 of this book, we introduced you to the principles and concepts of customer relationship management. Although this concept became widespread in the past, it was only fairly recently that it has again become one of the main themes in business. Philip Kotler, the well-known marketing academic, has always emphasised the exchange of value as an important part of marketing. These exchanges are in the form of transactions between the customer and the company. If a company is successful in satisfying the customer in terms of this value exchange in a consistent way, then it can create a relationship with that customer where these transactions take place regularly.

3.5.1 Reasons for Emphasis on Relationships and not Transactions

Many factors have led to this shift in emphasis to a relationship approach. Until a few years ago, many companies faced a situation where many markets were growing, where demand outstripped supply and where competition was not as intense as it is today. The situation is often far different now, with many markets in the mature phase, and facing overcapacity and oversupply. Since this means that finding new customers becomes increasingly difficult, companies have to take action to keep their good customers. Also, many businesses face the reality of having to keep a customer for a lengthy period before that customer becomes profitable. Customers, through better access to media and information, are more knowledgeable about alternative suppliers and products. The international focus on customer and value-added aspects has also led to customers being more demanding. These factors have reinforced the trend for companies to form stronger relationships with their customers.

3.5.2 The Payoff of Relationships and Good Service – Loyalty[12]

In order to reap the rewards of establishing a relationship, the company has to generate loyalty – and the benefits of loyalty to an organisation can be startling. In order to recoup the costs of acquiring a customer, many companies have to keep that customer for a number of years. In fact, only after a few years do many customers become profitable. If a company is busy 'churning' customers, then it may not be keeping them long enough for them to become profitable — and the company's performance suffers as a result. Loyal customers are more profitable, because spending by customers in most businesses tends to accelerate over time. In fact, customer spending should be managed in such a way that it is actually encouraged.

Another reason why loyal customers are more profitable is that customers learn to be more efficient as they learn about a business over time. They therefore do not waste time asking for services that the company does not provide. Furthermore, by learning about the company, both customers and the employees they interact with are more productive.

Referrals also are important long-term benefits of loyalty. For example, think of referrals that an automobile dealership can gain through a long-term relationship with a loyal customer. In fact, many customers who are referred are often of higher quality in terms of the profitability and longevity of the relationship than customers who respond to marketing communication efforts.

Lastly, loyal customers often provide the company with more profitability through price premiums than new customers do. By establishing a long-term relationship with a company, a customer gets better value and tends to be less price sensitive on individual product items than a new customer is.

Loyalty, built up through establishing a relationship, is attained only through customers perceiving a consistent delivery of service quality. Yet, customer service often fails to deliver this quality. Some reasons why customer service fails are discussed next.

3.5.3 Reasons Why Customer Service Fails

Many organisations do not understand how to practically implement customer service. Some of the biggest reasons why customer service fails are listed below:[13]

- **The market is not properly segmented:** The organisation wants to get its product or service to everyone in the world, but does not properly understand the market's needs.

- **The customer database is incomplete or non-existent:** Because of this, improvement in customer service is based on what the managers think is best, instead of what the customers want, i.e. customers' perceptions are disregarded.

- **The organisation is managed from the inside out:** The organisation uses a push strategy — it tells customers to use the product — as opposed to a pull strategy, where research is done to work out what customers need and want; the product or service is then developed; and, due to the need, customers will actively seek out the product or service.

- **All blame is shifted downward:** Front-line employees are blamed for any service failure, regardless of a lack of training and/or the failure of organisational systems, processes or structures.

- **Misunderstanding below the line of visibility:** Employees who are below the line of visibility (i.e. never in contact with customers) struggle to understand the need for customer service; however, these employees still have an important role to play in the delivery of exceptional customer service.

- **The focus is on attracting new customers as opposed to the retention of customers:** Little effort is made to keep the company's most profitable segment — its existing customers.
- **Dehumanised customers:** To many employees and managers, a customer does not have a face, which can lead to the customer becoming less human in their minds, and therefore less deserving of respect.

As mentioned earlier, there is a strong link among customer satisfaction, customer retention and customer loyalty. The extent of the customer's satisfaction with a product or service will determine its success in the market. It is therefore necessary to look at ways of measuring customer satisfaction.

3.6 Measuring Customer Satisfaction[14]

Since customer satisfaction is the objective of most successful companies, the service quality needs to be measured by how well they in fact satisfy their customers. There have been various efforts to measure overall customer satisfaction.

3.6.1 Benefits of Customer Satisfaction Surveys

Customer satisfaction surveys provide several worthwhile benefits, such as the following:

- **Customer feedback:** Such surveys provide a formal means of customer feedback to the organisation, which may identify existing and potential problems.
- **Show that the company cares:** Satisfaction surveys also convey the message to customers that the organisation cares about their well-being and values customer input concerning its operations.
- **Evaluating employee performance:** Satisfaction results are often utilised in evaluating employee performance for merit and compensation reviews and for sales management purposes, such as the development of sales training programmes.
- **Comparison purposes:** Survey results help a company to identify its own strengths and weaknesses, and where it stands in comparison to its competitors. When ratings are favourable, many organisations utilise the results in their corporate advertising.
- **Focus on customer needs:** Ultimately, the major advantage of customer satisfaction measurement is that it helps to secure an increased focus on

customer needs and to stimulate the work practices and processes used within the company.

However, the placement of customer feedback forms by some companies makes customers wonder if they really want the feedback. For example, some comment cards are often 'hidden' in magazines and are difficult to complete and return.

3.6.2 Problems in Measuring Customer Satisfaction

There are limits to interpreting any measure of customer satisfaction because of the following reasons:

- **Level of aspiration:** Satisfaction depends on and is relative to customers' level of aspiration or expectation. Less prosperous customers begin to expect more as they see the higher living standards of others.

- **Changes in levels of aspiration:** Aspiration levels tend to rise with repeated successes and fall with failures. Products considered satisfactory one day may not be satisfactory the next day, or vice versa. Years ago, most people were satisfied with a 21-inch colour TV that received three or four channels. But once they become accustomed to a large-screen HD model and enjoy all the options possible with digital satellite feed and a DVT, that old TV is never the same again.

- **Personal concept:** Customer satisfaction is a highly personal concept – and looking at the average satisfaction of a whole society does not provide a complete picture for evaluating effectiveness. At a minimum, some consumers are more satisfied than others. So, although efforts to measure satisfaction are useful, any evaluation of effectiveness has to be largely subjective.

Let us look at a few ways of measuring customer satisfaction.

3.6.3 Ways of Measuring Customer Satisfaction

The use of formal surveys has emerged as by far the best method of periodically assessing customer satisfaction. The surveys are not marketing tools, but information-gaining tools. Enough homework thus needs to be done before carrying out the actual survey.

After-sales surveys

After-sales surveys assess customer satisfaction while the service encounter is still fresh in the customer's mind. Consequently, the information reflects the organisation's recent performance, but may be biased by the customer's inadvertent attempt to minimise cognitive dissonance. After-sales surveys can also identify areas for improvement, and are seen as a proactive approach to assessing customer satisfaction. After-sales surveys attempt to contact every customer and allow the company to take corrective action if a customer is less than satisfied with his/her purchase decision. In South Africa, several motorcar dealers use this method after the purchase of a vehicle.

Mystery shopping

Mystery shopping is a form of non-customer research that measures individual employee service behaviour. As the name indicates, mystery shoppers are generally trained personnel who pose as customers and who shop unannounced at the business. The idea is to evaluate an individual employee during an actual service encounter. Mystery shoppers evaluate employees on a number of characteristics, such as the time it takes for the employee to acknowledge the customer, eye contact, appearance and other specific customer service factors. Results obtained from mystery shoppers are used as constructive employee feedback. Consequently, mystery shopping aids the business in coaching, training, evaluating and formally recognising its employees.

Customer satisfaction index (CSI)

One method that can be used is the customer satisfaction index (CSI), which is based on regular interviews with many customers. This index makes it possible to track changes in customer satisfaction measures over time and even allows comparison among companies. The questionnaire used must not be complicated and difficult to complete, in order to try and ensure a higher response rate. It must, however, still provide the correct data that is useful to the company. This means that it should be accurate and reliable. Questions asked of respondents vary and data can be collected by personal interviews or self-administered questionnaires. Many companies prefer to use short telephone or cellphone interviews.

The questionnaire should contain 'objective'-type questions where the customer has to 'rate' specific aspects about the organisation and its service or its products on a scale of, say, 1 to 5 or 1 to 10. The reason for providing a rating is that it gives respondents a way to express the importance they attach to various survey parameters. Respondents should be asked to give a weighting factor (e.g. on a scale of 1 to 5 or 1 to 10) for each requirement. This gives a better indication of the relative importance of each parameter towards overall customer satisfaction and makes it easier for organisations to prioritise their action plans by comparing the performance rating (scores) with importance rating (weighting).

SERVQUAL

Various methods have been suggested to measure service quality, the most well-known being that of the SERVQUAL instrument.[15] This instrument for measuring service quality is based on the differences between the perceptions and expectations of customers regarding the various dimensions of service quality, namely tangibles, responsiveness, reliability, empathy and assurance.[16] Statements are formulated, and based on these statements, the respondent is able to indicate both the expectation and the perception that they have of the specific dimension. The difference between the perceptions and expectations indicates the existence of a gap. In total there are a minimum of 21 statements that cover these 5 service quality dimensions.[17] This may vary depending on the industry in which the service quality is evaluated.

An example of a statement that can be used in a typical SERVQUAL used to evaluated lecturers can be seen below.[18]

	My EXPECTED LEVEL of services is:	My PERCEPTION of my lecturer's service is:
	LOW HIGH	LOW HIGH
The lecturer on this course inspires confidence	1 2 3 4 5 6 7	1 2 3 4 5 6 7

Despite its extensive use in measuring service quality, the SERVQUAL instrument is not without its criticis. Cronin and Taylor have specifically commented on the measurement of both the expectations and perceptions in the SERVQUAL instrument.[19] However, despite the criticisms that have been levelled against SERVQUAL, it remains an instrument that is used in all areas of business and industry, including the non-profit sector, so much so that its use has largely been "institutionalised".[20]

But how does measuring service quality affect relationship building? Measuring service quality indicates whether a gap exists between the customer's expectations and his/her perceptions. If the customer does not perceive that he is receiving a quality service from the organisation, he will not want to build a relationship with the organisation. SERVQUAL will indicate what type of actions management need to take to improve the quality, and thus the overall relationship with the customer.

3.7 Moments of Truth or Service Encounters[21]

The term 'moment of truth' was coined by Jan Carlzon, the president of Scandinavian Airline Systems (SAS), following a study commissioned by him to establish what SAS needed to do to improve its service. Carlzon used the phrase to rally the employees of SAS at a time when the airline industry was in dire economic straits. He convinced them that every contact between a customer and any employee of the airline constituted a moment of truth. In these brief encounters, he argued, the customer made up his/her mind about the quality of service and the quality of the product offered by SAS. Carlzon estimated there were 50 000 moments of truth in a given day in the SAS system — 50 000 moments of truth daily that had to be managed. He succeeded in taking SAS from near bankruptcy to profitability in less than two years.

The 'moment of truth' concept literally means that now is the time and the place when and where the organisation has the opportunity to demonstrate the quality of its services to the customer. It is a true moment of opportunity. In the next moment, the opportunity will be lost, the customer will have gone, and there are no easy ways of adding value to the perceived service quality. If a quality problem has occurred, it is too late to take corrective action. In order to do so, a new moment of truth has to be created. The marketer can, for example, actively contact the customer to correct a mistake or to at least explain why things have gone wrong. This is, of course, much more troublesome and probably less effective than a well-managed moment of truth.

It is important to emphasise the issue of remoteness. We must remember how customer perceptions are formed and can be influenced. These perceptions are directly tied in with the customer's opinion of the service offered by a company. We must also remember that customers view service as they perceive it, not according to reality. Hence, the moment of truth is not only the actual service that the customer receives face to face, but could also include contact by telephone or by post. The point to remember is that the moment of truth is any contact customers have where they are able to form an impression about an organisation.

An organisation may not have 50 000 moments of truth a day, but it is probably safe to say that there are several hundred that occur every day, and every one of them must be managed to achieve a positive outcome if the organisation hopes to renew customer loyalty on a sustained basis. It is important to remember that a moment of truth is not, in itself, positive or negative. It is how the service encounter is managed that will turn the moment of truth into a positive or negative experience for the customer.

Also, keep in mind that a moment of truth does not necessarily have to involve human contact. The customer experiences a moment of truth when he/she drives into your parking lot. Are there sufficient parking spaces? Are the grounds clean and attractive? Is the entrance to your business easy to find? Are signs placed logically, and are they easy to read? All of these are potential moments of truth, and they happen even before you have a chance to perform for your customer.

The major contributing factor to the moment of truth and the impression formed is the customer's interaction with front-line employees; in other words, those who deal with or have personal contact with the customers on a day-to-day basis. These include, for example, the receptionist, the petrol attendant, the switchboard operator and the parts salesperson.

Moments of truth are therefore crucial to perceived quality of service and, as such, can be regarded as a major contributor to the service performance of a company.

Some moments of truth for an airline

- The customer calls the airline for information.
- The customer books the flight with the airline representative.
- The customer arrives at the airline's airport counter.
- The customer waits in the queue.
- The ticket agent invites the customer to the counter.
- The ticket agent processes payment and issues the ticket.
- The customer starts looking for the departure gate.
- The gate agent welcomes the customer to the flight and validates the boarding pass.
- The customer waits in the departure lounge for the flight to depart.
- The boarding agent takes the customer's ticket and invites the customer on board.
- The customer boards the aircraft and is greeted by the flight attendant.
- The customer looks for his or her assigned seat.
- The customer looks for a place to stow carry-on luggage.
- The customer takes his or her seat.
- The customer experiences all aspects of the flight (making up a whole series of moments of truth).
- The customer collects his/her baggage after the flight is over.

Often 'unexpected' services will cause the customer to positively evaluate the organisation's product or service. Customers evaluate a store, for example, on their perceptions of that store's service. In this case, the service of the store depends on the employees working in the store. Employees play an important part in the customer's perception of the service. Customer evaluations of service are often based on the way in which employees provide the service, not just the outcome. Consider the following example:

The way in which employees provide service

A customer goes to a large store to return a product that is not working properly. In one case, the company policy requires the employee to ask the customer for a receipt, test whether the product is not working, ask a manager whether a refund can be provided, complete the paperwork and finally refund the customer the amount paid for the product in cash.

In a second case, the store employee simply asks the customers how much he/she had paid for the product and refunds the cash.

The outcome is the same in both cases — but the customer is more satisfied in the second case than in the first.

3.7.1 Types of Service Encounters

Customers experience three main types of service encounters.

Remote encounter

A *remote* encounter occurs when there is no human contact. Examples of this include the use of automated teller machines (ATMs), or direct mail methods. Since more and more services are being delivered through technology, this type of encounter is becoming increasingly important. In these encounters, the tangible evidence of service and the quality of the process itself (the process dimension of service quality) become the basis for judging the quality of the service.

Telephone or cellphone encounter

The *telephone* (or cellphone) encounter is, for many businesses, the most frequent type of encounter with end customers. Important criteria for judging this encounter include tone of voice, an employee's knowledge and his/her effectiveness in handling customer issues. The popularity of call centres has emphasised the importance of this type of encounter for many companies.

Direct contact

An important encounter is *direct contact* (face to face). This is a complex way of trying to establish service quality, because both verbal and non-verbal behaviour need to be considered.

3.7.2 Ingredients of a Moment of Truth

The ingredients of the moment of truth are the service context, frame of reference and congruence.

Service context

All encounters between the organisation and the customer occur in a specific setting or service context. The service context can be described as *the collective impact of all the social, physical and psychological elements that happen during the moment of truth*. The service context that is created is the overall effect of the environment created by the attitude and approach of all employees as they assist customers.

A good way of illustrating the service context is by using an example of a car rental company.

Service context: A car rental company

There is a big difference in the service context of a car rental company when you initially check a car out as compared to the service context when you bring the car back to check it in. When a rented car is checked out, there is usually a big push to create added revenue for the rental company. Agents suggest a larger vehicle 'for only two rand more per day', or they try to sell expensive insurance, because the customer is responsible for the total cost of the vehicle in case of an accident. The keys to a spotless, usually late-model car are presented and the customer is invariably wished a nice day.

However, compare the service context of the check-out process with the check-in process. You arrive at the parking lot and park the car. A voice on a recorder repeatedly booms out: 'Leave your keys in the car and proceed to the check-in desk.' The company and the customer perceive obviously different service contexts from their respective frames of reference. The company considers the service complete when the bill is paid. To the customer, billing and checking in are a nuisance. The customer perceives that the service is over when he or she gets out of the car. The rest is viewed as red tape for the company's benefit.

Rarely does anyone enquire whether the car was satisfactory or in good operating condition. No-one asks whether the business trip was successful, or if

---

there is any additional service they can provide. There are no 'value-added' benefits to make the car rental company stand out from the others in business. In short, the customer walks away with a bill, and that's about it. Customers are not made to feel special.

The check-in point seems to be an ideal moment to make a favourable impression, but, this does not happen.

Frame of reference

Both the customer and the service employee approach the moment of truth encounter from the individual's frame of reference, which then totally dominates their thinking processes, attitudes, feelings and behaviour. The frame of reference has a powerful effect upon the meaning that individuals assign to the moment of truth.

Some of the inputs that create the frame of reference may be automatic, e.g. both people may speak English and both represent social norms and customs with which they are mutually familiar. Some inputs to the customer's fame of reference may, however, differ from inputs that create the service employee's frame of reference. When that happens, the two individuals view the moment of truth encounter from very different perspectives. It is important to note that frames of reference can change in an instant. As the customer perceives that a need is being met or not being met, the frame of reference filter changes. Along with it, the customer's perception of the moment of truth changes. The same is true for the person who is providing the service or product for the customer.

Among the many possible inputs that help create the customer's frame of reference are:

♦ past experience with the business or similar business;
♦ beliefs about the business;
♦ expectations formed by previous experiences;
♦ attitudes, beliefs, ethnic norms and values that have formed during the customer's lifetime; and
♦ recommendations or warnings from other customers.

Among those inputs that help create the service employee's frame of reference are:

♦ what the company has told the employee to do;
♦ rules and regulations set for service employees and customers;
♦ the employee's level of emotional maturity;
♦ expectations of customer behaviour based on past experience;
♦ attitudes, beliefs and values formed during the employee's lifetime; and

◆ the tools and resources, or the lack thereof, used to deliver the service or product.

Congruence

One of the key concepts of the moment of truth is the need for congruence, i.e. a working compatibility among the three factors of context, the customer's frame of reference and the employee's frame of reference. This means that there must be agreement at the moment of truth. If the inputs to the customer's frame of reference and that of the service employee differ greatly from each other, then the moment of truth could be adversely affected. There must be some alignment of the customer's frame of reference with that of the service employee in order for the moment of truth to be positive for the company on a consistent basis, and both must be congruent with the service context.

When there is a lack of congruence, the probability of a satisfactory result is reduced. This is often the case when a service problem occurs. Customers will describe their own actions as completely reasonable, rational and polite. Service employees will describe their own behaviour in the same say. However, when the customer describes the behaviour of the service employee, the employee's behaviour is described in terms of impatience, exasperation and disrespect for the customer. The service employee, on the other hand, describes the customer's behaviour as arrogant, demanding and rude. Often the truth lies somewhere between the two extremes, but we can see that the underlying cause is that the frames of reference are mismatched, owing to the different inputs of the employee and customer.

3.7.3 Cycle of Service

Moments of truth do not happen in a haphazard way. They usually occur in a logical, measurable sequence. By placing the moments of truth in their logical sequence, the organisation can identify the exact encounters for which front-line and other employees are responsible. Once the logical sequence of the moments of truth has been determined, then the cycle of service has been created. The cycle of service, depicted in figure 3.2 shows the service as the customer experiences it.

A cycle of service is a map of the moments of truth as they are experienced by customers. The cycle of service is activated every time a customer comes into contact with the business. Just as there are hundreds of moments of truth in a given business day, so are there many cycles of service. The value of mapping cycles of service for the various departments in the organisation is that one is able to look through the customer's eyes and evaluate the business from the customer's perspective.

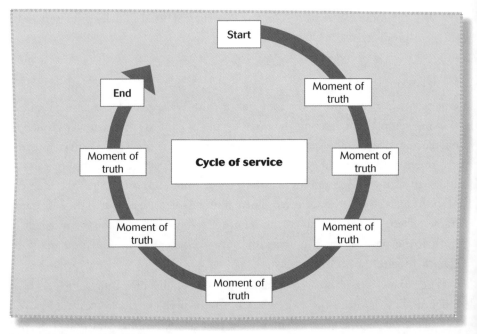

Figure 3.2 Cycle of Service

Mapping out cycles of service is best done by the manager or supervisor and the employees who are directly involved in delivering service for that particular cycle. It is worth repeating, however, that it must be identified from the customer's point of view. Often, it is only the customer who perceives the full picture of the service experience, while managers and employees are only aware of their part of the cycle. The result is that managers or employees in a section may think they have provided good service, while the customer perceives the whole service experience and may decide that the service has been bad.

A second reason for illustrating service encounters in a cyclical way is to separate the important moments of truth from the critical moments of truth. While all of the moments of truth in a service encounter are important, there is usually a smaller number that are of such importance to the success of the business that they are called the *critical moments of truth*.

When the cycles of service for the major operations of the organisation have been created, it will be possible to spot those moments of truth that, if not managed positively, will almost certainly lead to customer dissatisfaction, loss of loyalty to your service or product, and possible loss of the customer's business. These are the critical moments of truth. It is imperative that people in the organisation whose work centres around these key encounters with customers be equipped with the skills required for positive outcomes. For example, a critical moment of truth for most businesses happens when one of the organisation's systems fails, as one of them certainly will from time to time. At that precise moment, the company's service reputation is at stake. When this happens, it will take a quick-thinking person to make the situation right again with the customer. The 'recovery' record for responding to systems failures is one of the hallmarks of credibility for the service-managed business. The critical moments of truth, if left unmanaged, invariably lead to a loss of customer confidence. Once customer confidence is lost, the loss of loyalty and repeat business soon follows.

The cycle of service is therefore the chain of events made up of particular moments of truth or encounters that customers go through as they experience a service. Customers, in their exposure to the cycle, are usually concerned about their needs and expectations. The company, on the other hand, is often more concerned with the systems that are in place to handle any customer interaction. It is only the customer, however, who actually experiences the full cycle of service. This means that the overall result may still be customer dissatisfaction, even though each service provider feels it treated the customer correctly at its particular moment of truth.

The organisation must ensure that it is managing the moments of truth through the cycle of service so as to deliver excellent service. If the encounters or moments of truth are not managed, the customer's needs will be met only some of the time. This means that the organisation can hope to achieve only mediocrity in terms of service quality, since it will win some encounters and lose others.

Managing the moments of truth implies establishing the customer's expectations at each critical moment of truth and then deciding on how to ensure that service is delivered to meet expectations. Aspects that need to be considered at each encounter include skills, competencies, attitudes, time, knowledge, equipment, decision-making capability and authority.

3.7.4 Sources of Satisfaction/Dissatisfaction in the Moment of Truth

Research has identified four factors that can lead to satisfaction or dissatisfaction in terms of the moments of truth. These four are:[22]

- **Recovery:** This includes all incidents where the service delivery system has failed somehow and an employee has to respond to customer complaints. The way the employee responds, in terms of content and form, leads to a favourable or unfavourable memory of the incident for the customer.

- **Adaptability:** The second factor is how adaptable the service delivery system is when the customer has special needs or requests. Customers often perceive that something special is being done for them based on their needs, or they are frustrated by the unwillingness of the company to adapt to or accommodate their needs.

- **Spontaneity:** The third factor encompasses pleasant surprises for the customer, such as special attention to something being done that was not requested. Unsatisfactory incidents often include negative or rude behaviour towards the customer.

- **Coping:** The fourth factor revolves around the customer being unco-operative, where the service provided could do nothing that would satisfy the customer or lead to him/her being pleased about the encounter. Coping is the behaviour of the employees in handling these 'problem' customers.

These four factors and the specific behaviours for each that lead to either positive or negative encounters are summarised in table 3.2.

Table 3.2 General Service Behaviours for the Four Factors

Factor	Do	Don't
Recovery	Acknowledge the problem Explain its causes Apologise Compensate/upgrade Lay out options Take responsibility	Ignore the customer Blame the customer Leave the customer to 'fend for him-/herself' Downgrade Act as if nothing is wrong 'Pass the buck'
Adaptability	Recognise the seriousness of the need Acknowledge Anticipate Attempt to accommodate Adjust the system Explain rules/policies Take responsibility	Ignore Promise, but fail to follow through Embarrass the customer Laugh at the customer 'Pass the buck'
Spontaneity	Take time Be attentive Anticipate needs Listen Provide information Show empathy	Exhibit impatience Ignore Yell/laugh/swear Discriminate
Coping	Listen Try to accommodate Explain Let go of the customer (i.e. stop dealing with the customer)	Let the customer's dissatisfaction affect others

3.8 Servicescapes[23]

After analysing the moments of truth, we need to understand what a company can do to ensure that the service experience is pleasant for the customer. The actual physical facility where the service is performed, delivered and consumed is referred to as the *servicescape*. For example, in terms of Disney, the servicescape would be Disney World itself – it can be considered as the stage where everything happens. In the example of Woolworths, the actual store facility would be the servicescape where the company's service is experienced.

The servicescape forms part of the physical evidence that companies need to provide the customer with as cues for its service quality.

Elements of the servicescape that affect service include both exterior and interior attributes. Exterior attributes are visible on the outside of the facility, while interior ones are visible inside the facility. Table 3.3 gives a brief view of the elements contained in both the exterior and interior of the facility.

Table 3.3 Elements of Servicescapes

Facility exterior	Facility interior
Exterior design and colour scheme	Interior design and colour scheme
Signage	Equipment
Parking	Signage
Landscape	Layout
Surrounding environment	Air quality/temperature

To elaborate on the factors listed above, for exterior facility factors, one must keep in mind that not all these factors can be controlled by the company, for example, the owner of a shop in a mall does not have the power to change the design of the parking lot; however, if a customer struggles to find parking outside the shop, this will still fall under the overall service cycle.

The interior facility factors can be managed much more extensively by the company, which can improve the interior facility and by so doing still improve the overall impression a customer has. For example, after struggling to find parking, a store with soft lighting, gentle music and air-conditioning may be a very welcome place to be for the same customer who has struggled to find parking.

Let us consider the example of a sporting event. South Africa has already successfully hosted many top world events, such as the Rugby World Cup and the Cricket World Cup. What are some of the elements of the servicescape that were considered?

Clearly, there are many, but some of the more important ones include parking, the stadium exteriors, the ticket sales areas, the entrances to the facilities, the seating, the restrooms within the stadium, the concession areas and the playing fields themselves. Each of these, working in conjunction with the others, can give the customers the evidence needed as to what service experience to expect.

3.8.1 Roles Played by the Servicescape

We mentioned above that the servicescape is important in providing physical evidence of service. It can play many roles in this regard.

Package the offer

The first is to package the offer. This can give an indication, through the external image, of what the consumer can expect inside. This is often the initial impression and is a moment of truth for the customer, especially for a newly established organisation trying to build a specific image. This appearance can be extended to the actual dress of the staff and other aspects related to their outward appearance.

Facilitator

The second role that the servicescape can fill is that of facilitator in terms of helping in the performance of people in that environment. Through good design, the flow of activities can be improved, facilitating goal achievement. Where good design can make the experience a pleasure for the customer, bad design can lead to frustration and even actual discomfort — one only has to think of some of the airline seats that passengers are forced to endure in the name of efficiency and profits!

Aid in socialisation

The servicescape design can also aid in socialisation, in that both customers and employees can better understand their expected roles, behaviours and relationships. By absorbing the position, appearance and placement of the surroundings, employees can deduce what expectations the company has of them. The design can also help to establish, for customers and staff, exactly what types of interactions are encouraged. For example, consider the changes that have occurred in the servicescape related to booksellers. Until recently, browsing through books and magazines was actively discouraged, and customers were forced to make their choices standing up, as there was nowhere for them to sit. Staff members were placed behind a desk, and the whole feel was unfriendly and Spartan. The servicescape in many successful booksellers has changed dramatically. The customer is encouraged to browse, and the product is available for easy handling. Comfortable chairs and sofas are provided so that the customer can relax and go though the product at leisure. Many stores now even provide coffee shops within the store to encourage social interaction and further improve the experience. Staff members are encouraged to roam the aisles and socialise with the customers, and provide information as needed.

Differentiation

The last role that the servicescape can fulfil is differentiation of the company from its competitors. As alluded to above, changes in the servicescape can be used to reposition a company or even attract new market segments. For example, by adding a gourmet section with detailed information and a wider range of product choices, a food retailer could expand its target market and attract new customers. Consider the launch of Cinema Privé by Nu Metro, where the whole servicescape of watching movies has been changed to one of a more pleasant experience through luxury facilities, a bar service and special treatment that avoids the crush of the masses at peak times.

The servicescape can perform either one or all of these roles simultaneously, but in order to ensure complete management of the service experience, the marketer needs not only to consider physical facilities through the servicescape, but also to look at the culture of the organisation.

A few common examples of poor service (also known as the sins of service) that often lead to upset customers are provided.

3.9 Poor Service (Sins of Service)

It has often been said that 'little things' — the details — affect the customer's perception of quality of service. Most customers are appreciative when they know a company is making a real effort to make things right. The slipping of standards with respect to little aspects can be a death blow to customers' perceptions of service quality. We can identify a number of these 'sins' of service.

Apathy

The worst form of apathy is when service employees convince customers that they really do not care about the customers' problems. Apathy is an indication of an employee who has lost interest in customers, and when service employees stop caring, they should be replaced.

Brushing customers off

This is when service employees try to dispose of the customers, usually because they have something else to do, especially close to lunch time and closing time.

Coolness towards customers

Here the service employee is overly formal, unsmiling and officious. The service context in this situation is perceived by the customer as cold and uncaring.

Treating customers with condescension

This is shown when service employees talk down to customers, use words that the customer cannot understand, or shout at customers who cannot speak a certain language well.

Robot syndrome

This occurs when service employees become so used to the routine that they do everything in the same way, day after day. Many times, service employees do not even realise that the customers are there, do not acknowledge their presence, and often speak to the social class of the customer rather than directly to the customer. How many times have you tried to pay a bill and the person behind the counter hasn't acknowledged you as a customer? Employees like this ignore the face-to-face customer contact that is so critical to positive service perceptions.

Following the rules

This occurs when the rules and procedures of a company are created more for the organisation's convenience than for the convenience of customers. Often, systems and procedures are established by employees in an organisation who are far removed from the face-to-face customer's point of view. In terms of CRM, the rules must be designed from the customer's point of view. This will ensure that the company is perceived as service oriented.

The customer turnaround

This is a way of disposing of customers by directing them to another department in the organisation. How many times have you been transferred from one department to another, while nothing is done to deal with your complaint?

By ensuring that a service system that is customer-focused exists in your organisation, the common examples of bad service can be minimised.

3.10 Key Success Factors of Service Management

Service management should be a total organisational approach so as to ensure that superior service is one of the driving forces of your business. The problem that businesses think they face is that a choice must be made among the three elements, namely, product quality, service quality and cost containment. In order to develop a truly service-oriented organisation, four key success factors of service management must be understood, as shown in figure 3.3.

Employees have a big effect on the process of providing service. Marketers, therefore, need to be reminded that it is not the problem itself, but the way in which the problem is handled that distinguishes good service from bad service. If the customer has been handled in the correct way, the customer will come back to the store and the marketer has succeeded in establishing a long-term relationship. Surprisingly, those customers who have a problem with a supplier, and whose complaint is resolved, stay even more loyal than those who never complained in the first place!

Customers are eager to evaluate service quality when an unexpected event occurs. For example, if customers have a problem locating certain merchandise in a store, they would like some guidance in finding merchandise. Employees must be equipped and trained to help such customers.

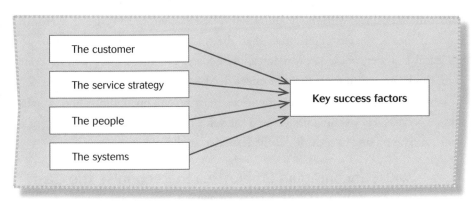

Figure 3.3 Key Success Factors

Let us now consider each of the factors in figure 3.3.

3.10.1 Key Success Factors

The customer

All of the processes in an organisation revolve around the customer. Customers must be identified and understood. Service management is based on a customer-centred organisation that makes the customer's needs and expectations the central focus of the business. The underlying principle to keep mind is that *the customer always comes first*.

The service strategy

The service strategy directs the attention of the people in the organisation toward the real priorities of the customer. It has two key parts, the *official corporate commitment to service*, and the *service promise* to customers. The service strategy becomes the basis for future decisions about the company, its service and its operations.

The people

The managers of service-oriented organisations must help to ensure that service employees focus on meeting the needs of the customer. Effective front-line employees are able to maintain this focus of attention by being aware of the need to provide the service in such a way that customers perceive it as being superior. This makes customers want to tell others about the service and come back for more.

The systems

All employees in an organisation must work within the systems that organise the running of a business. Customers must work their way through these systems in order to do business with the organisation. These systems must be designed for the convenience of the customer rather than the convenience of the organisation. The physical facilities, policies, procedures, methods of communication and processes must all be geared to meet the customer's needs.

It was mentioned earlier that employees must be equipped and trained in customer service. They should understand the value of each customer to the organisation, and be trained to provide excellent service at all times.

3.10.2 Encouraging Employees to Recognise the Cash Value of Each Customer

One way of underlining to employees the importance of keeping customers is for management to stress the cash value of each customer. Consider the following example:

The cash value of each customer

A fast-food pizza chain in the US has calculated that a single customer who comes back regularly over a period of ten years is worth $5 000 to the chain. Employees of the pizza store now recognise that what they do or say can have far-reaching financial consequences beyond the profit of one pizza. Everybody at the store, from the telephone operator to the delivery person, now knows how important it is to ensure that each and every customer is satisfied.

In chapters 1 and 2, the lifetime value of each customer (CLV) was highlighted. The lifetime value is the same as the cash value mentioned above.

The CLV is a formula that expresses a customer's present value in monetary terms. CLV consists of three factors, as shown in table 3.4:

Table 3.4 Factors of CLV[24]

	Recency	Frequency	Volume
Definition	Date of last purchase	Average number of purchases a year	Average spend per purchase
To increase CLV	Purchase should be recent	Purchases should be frequent	Spend per purchase should be high

The CLV is based on the combination of the above factors, e.g. if the customer purchased a large amount (volume), once (frequency) two years ago (recency), CLV will be low, since both frequency and recency are low. From the above, the importance of building and maintaining a long-term relationship with the customer becomes more important.

Other factors that should be taken into account when measuring the lifetime value of a customer include: 1) the period of time over which CLV should be measured; 2) the interest rate to be used to determine the present value of the customer; and 3) all the costs related to the customer that should be taken into account, e.g. costs of merchandise sold, services provided and maintenance.[25]

3.11 Elements of Great Service

To be truly exceptional, customer service should lead to positive word of mouth (WOM) communications.[26] This is more important than ever. It is no longer just a case of a customer complaining about bad service, because most customers are technologically savvy nowadays, and if a customer does or doesn't like a service provided, he/she can discuss it in his/her blog or start a group on Facebook. He/she may even start a webpage where anyone searching the Internet for the company's name might find a page describing his/her pleasant/unpleasant service experience, which might be easier to find than the company's own website. Positive WOM is therefore more important than ever.

3.11.1 Steps to Remarkable Customer Service

Adapted from the practical experience of Joel Spolsky, of the software company Fog Creek, the following are practical steps to exceptional customer service:

◢ Fix everything two ways

When a customer has a complaint, it cannot be ignored. Efforts should be given to finding a solution to the customer's immediate problem. Once the complaint is resolved, the second way to fix the problem is to try to ensure that the same mistake doesn't happen twice, therefore the root of the problem must be identified and solved throughout the business.

◢ Think laterally to avoid customer offence

Sometimes a problem can be quite easily solved by the customer him-/herself, especially in the case where a customer has phoned into a help desk. If the problem is solved without the customer having to return the product, it will save the customer time and effort, which they will greatly appreciate. However, if the problem is simple to solve, the customer might take offence at your suggestions, e.g. suggesting that an electrical appliance is not plugged in. Try to think laterally to solve the problem without offending the customer, e.g. suggest that the customer blows the dust off the plug, thereby ensuring that the customer checks that the appliance is plugged in, without insulting his/her intelligence.

◢ Make customers into fans

People make mistakes, and it is almost impossible to provide perfect service every time, first time round; however, complete recovery from service failure can sometimes leave a much bigger impact on customer satisfaction and positive WOM than good service the first time round. This is because customers expect the service to go well, and will not necessarily think anything of it when it does; however, customers often do not expect their complaints to be resolved, and will be pleasantly surprised if they are. This is not to say a company should strive to fail the first time round, since customers still prefer a certain amount of consistency. However, when things do go wrong, service recovery processes should be set in place. The following steps are examples of these processes and should be practised by everyone in the company from the top down.

◢ Service employees must seem eager to solve problems

Customers should not have to search for a salesperson; salespeople need to be available to the client, and must be seen to be keen to solve the problem.[27]

Take the blame

In many instances, a service employee may actually blame the customer, which is even worse if the fault truly does not lie with the customer. Most customers just want someone to take responsibility for the inconvenience caused by the service failure. Irate customers are often a result of service failure followed by blame shifting or further service failure. When a service employee takes the blame (even when it is not directly his/her fault) it has an emotionally calming effect on customers.[28]

Memorise useful phrases

Many service employees do not know what to say to calm a customer after service failure, and a few simple phrases can be memorised to help the process. The following are good examples: 'I'm sorry', 'It's my fault', 'Can I offer you the following to make up for your loss?' 'Please tell me everything that happened so that I can ensure it never happens again.' These phrases may not be easy to say, but perhaps when faced with the prospect of a happy customer in comparison to an angry customer, the happy customer does seem a better choice.

Often the problem here is with managers. Managers need to have the same attitude towards their customers that they expect their employees to have. However, many managers may understand that having a customer focus is beneficial, but at the same time might have the attitude that they are in some way above the customer and want to control the customer. This can can create a problem of attitude, since the manager, just as much as the service employee, needs to 'serve' the customer.[29]

Practise puppetry

Service employees need to understand that the customer's anger is not necessarily directed at them personally. Often the customer does not come into contact with the person responsible for the service failure, but the customer sees the company as a whole and for this reason will take out his/her frustration on the nearest representative of the company. One approach is to have the service employee visualise him-herself as a puppet and a puppet master in a puppet show. As the puppet master, he/she needs to try to discover what would be the best thing for the puppet to say in order to appease or please the customer. This way, the employee is not party to the argument, and can learn not to take the customer's behaviour personally.[30]

Go the extra mile

Exceptional service employees do that little something extra.[31] It may just be a small gesture, but it can mean the difference between good and exceptional service, and lead to very positive WOM. For example, if a store is out of stock (because of a delivery failure), the shop assistant could phone other stores in the vicinity and have a product immediately delivered. A good service employee will value a customer's time, realising that time is not only money, but is also keeping a customer away from places he/she would rather be, e.g. at home with his/her family.

Honour ceremonial expectations

Certain companies offer loyalty cards to offer the customer special services. The services promised should be delivered, because even if the other service offered by the company is exceptional, if the service provider fails to offer what is promised, the customer may still be disappointed.

Greed will get you nowhere

The responsibility should not all fall on the shoulders of the service employees; the company needs to put certain processes into place to help the service employee, even if they cost the company money. For example, having a 'no questions asked' return policy helps the service employee provide something of value to the customer, and with such a policy, the customer loses the feeling of helplessness, making the likelihood of an irate customer very slim, and finally leading to more positive WOM. What the company loses from returns it will gain back from referrals.[32]

Provide a performance guarantee

A guarantee removes much of the risk from purchasing a new product or a product that a customer has purchased before, but which has failed. There are a number of situations in which providing a guarantee can differentiate a company from its competitors: when you have a new product, when you have received negative publicity, when the product is complex or technical, when the product is not sold face to face, after a service failure and when the risk of loss is high.[33]

Give customer service people a career path

Much of the above cannot be achieved without the co-operation of service employees. By providing customer service people with a career path, the benefits to a company will be two-fold. Firstly, the company will be able to attract the best candidate for the job; and secondly, the company will benefit from a lower staff turnover. The career path needs to have value to service employees. For example, after two years in customer service, the company could offer to assist them to further their studies and promise them management positions after certain targets are met. These must also be realistic; it will not help if a company makes empty promises.[34]

Make sure something's in it for the employees

Good service employees understand that building a long-term relationship with a client will benefit them,[35] because they know that if the client comes back into the store, they will likely be there again and will have to deal with that client. So if the client was dealt with fairly or received exceptionally good service, it will be much easier to deal with that client in the future; however, if the client was treated badly, there is the possibility that he/she will not return, and even if he/she does return, in all likelihood he/she will be much more difficult to deal with.

3.11.2 Customer Service Process Model

Manufacturing industries put a lot of effort into in-depth design of process models; however, most practitioners in the service industry do not give this much thought.[36] Implementing a process model is another way by which service employees can be given a very clear understanding of how to provide excellent service. Figure 3.4 is an example of a service process model for a restaurant.

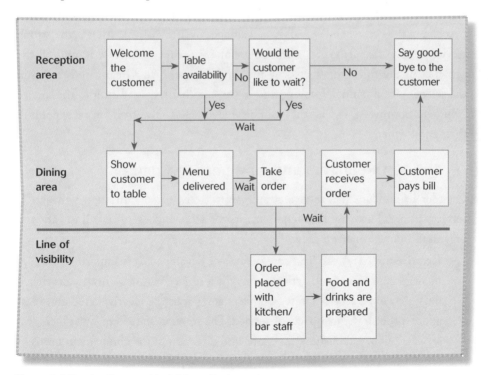

Figure 3.4 Service Process Model for a Restaurant

The line of visibility represents everything the customer can see. This is not to say that service can be below par under the line of visibility, but it does help to give service employees a good overview of the service process from the customer's point of view. Each block represents an event in the process. Arrows show the sequence of events, while arrows labelled 'Wait' represent the passing of time. Arrows can also be labelled with time spans; this will assist the service employee in understanding how long the process should preferably take.

3.12 Managing the Service Culture: Internal Service

A service culture can be said to exist in an organisation when a service orientation and an interest in customers are the most important norms within the organisation. Many companies have set the objective of being customer-centric, but few seem to have really instilled the culture in the organisation so that it becomes the lifeblood of the organisation. A corporate culture is *the set of common norms and values shared by people in the organisation.*[37] In common language, it can be described as the internal climate in the organisation. It is important to manage it, because a service culture could be a basis for a sustainable competitive advantage. Southwest Airlines in the USA has been one of the few airlines that has been profitable consistently over the last 40 years, and one of its advantages over the competition is the strong service culture that it has. Top management takes care to nurture it, and all the activities of the firm are affected by the service imperative. Great care is taken in the selection of potential employees to make sure that they will fit into the service culture of Southwest, so that they will be able to be effective from an early point in their employment.[38]

3.12.1 Requirements for a Service Culture

In order to implement a service strategy effectively, the organisation will need a service culture. There are four requirements for achieving a service culture, and the organisation must manage these.[39]

 Requirement 1: A service strategy must be developed. It is important that top management wants and actively aims for a service culture. This means that it must develop a service strategy. This strategy must be clearly stated and must address the strategic aspects of service. The mission statement must include a service vision, establishing the scope and direction of the company in terms of service delivery. The service concepts, therefore, will have to be clearly spelled out – what will be done, for whom and how, as well as the benefits that are to be offered. Resource management — human and otherwise — must be guided by the service strategy, as it is an important part of the service culture. The ways of measuring performance also have to reflect the objectives in terms of

the service strategy, and should measure not only efficiency, but also effectiveness.

Requirement 2: All aspects of the organisational structure must reflect the service strategy and processes. This is important, because the more complex the organisational structure, the more difficult it is to deliver good service consistently. The organisational structure of most retail banks in South Africa makes it problematic for them to deliver on their customer service excellence objectives. What is needed is quick and flexible decision making, and co-operation among the different departments in a company in order to deliver good service consistently. The implications of this for authority and decision making for front-line employees must be carefully considered. The identification of all customers, both external and internal, must be the basis of the structure decisions. This also means that managers have to understand their roles as facilitators of performance and in providing support for the front-line staff. The design of operational systems, work flows and routines has to be done with the customers' needs and expectations in mind, and the use of information technology is an opportunity to make the sharing of the customer culture a reality.

Requirement 3: A service-oriented leadership must be established. Members of management must support the service initiative in word and deed in order to maintain a service culture. This includes the roles they take as leaders in their teams, and how they act and speak. It is important that there should be no ambiguity about the service emphasis and the kind of behaviour expected of employees. It is especially important for the top manager of the company to speak continuously about service excellence and give strong support to it. When Toyota launched its Toyota Touch service initiative, it was supported and launched by the top executive at the time — Brand Pretorius. The idea is that management must guide the staff as to the correct set of values and attitudes to have, through visible leadership and coaching.

Requirement 4: The knowledge and attitudes needed for good service must be created through service training. This is an important part of internal marketing, which will be discussed in detail in a later chapter. The more knowledgeable employees are about the operations, the customer relationships and the expectations that exist, both in terms of the customer and themselves, the more likely they are to understand what is needed and why it is needed. This assumes that all the necessary information as explained in Requirement 1 is understood by all concerned.

3.12.2 Behavioural Code

Service employees need to understand what is expected of them, therefore training should be provided so that employees have a clear understanding of what constitutes great service. This can be assisted by providing a code of conduct for employees, and the following are good examples of how service employees should strive to behave on a daily basis:[40]

- **Only speak well of customers:** Service employees can get into the habit of competing for who has the worst customer, leading to a culture in which the customer is seen as the enemy. This is not beneficial to providing exceptional customer service; rather, employees need to see customers in a positive light, so that they *want* to help them, instead of *having* to.

- **Only speak well of competitors:** Feuding should be discouraged, and from the service employees' point of view, the focus should be on improving the company, not on one-upping the competition.

- **No temper tantrums:** Employees should be discouraged from phone slamming, swearing and generally poor behaviour. They need to realise that their negative behaviour has a chain reaction on all around them.

- **Speak to managers about issues:** When employees have a problem, they need to be able to speak openly and freely with their supervisors, i.e. a culture of open communication should be established.

- **Teamwork:** Offering assistance when other associates are in need should be encouraged; this also applies to supervisors.

3.12.3 Corporate Commitment

Exceptional service needs a commitment from the entire organisation in order to be successful. Goodman[41] states the following as necessary elements of corporate commitment:

- **Commitment is worth more than the paper it is written on:** Raymond Ackerman often uses the expression 'The customer is king'. This is an excellent slogan; however, to have any true value, it needs to be practised constantly.

- **Commitment needs to flow from the top down:** Managers and owners of businesses need to practise what they preach; they also need to invest time and money in exceptional service.

- **Commitment to service needs to become entrenched:** Exceptional service quality needs to be sustained; and service employees need to be continually reminded of the benefits of exceptional service, not only to the enterprise, but to each service employee as an individual.

◤ **Commitment to service needs to be properly compensated:** To ensure the above, the benefits promised to service employees should not only be stated, but actually delivered.

3.13 Summary

In this chapter, the various factors in customer service that influence the building of customer relationships were discussed. Service quality was highlighted, with specific reference to the link among relationships, quality service and customer loyalty. A few methods for measuring customer satisfaction were discussed. The moments of truth concept, or service encounters, formed a large part of the discussion of quality, as well as the cycle of service as experienced by customers when they interact with an organisation. The impacts of servicescapes were highlighted. Numerous practical applications of service quality were highlighted throughout the chapter. Lastly, we discussed the importance of a service culture to an organisation being able to achieve its service goals.

Discussion questions

1. Explain and illustrate the nature of customer service.
2. Explain, with the aid of practical examples, the quality outcomes when consumers compare the service they expect with the actual service they receive.
3. Discuss the different types of customer expectations and highlight the factors influencing service expectations.
4. Explain the dimensions used by consumers when evaluating service quality.
5. Illustrate the link among relationships, quality service and customer loyalty.
6. What are the benefits of customer satisfaction surveys and the problems in measuring customer satisfaction?
7. Explain, with the aid of practical examples, four methods of measuring customer satisfaction.
8. Discuss the moments of truth or service encounters for a bank under the following headings:
   ◆ the meaning of moments of truth or service encounters
   ◆ types of service encounters in a bank
   ◆ ingredients of a moment of truth
   ◆ sources of satisfaction/dissatisfaction in the moment of truth.
9. Discuss what aspects of the servicescape you would consider, in terms of managing the physical evidence of service, if you were the owner of a private

educational institution teaching degree programmes under a licence agreement with a major university.

10. Briefly explain the key success factors in service management that should be implemented to ensure that superior service is provided in the whole organisation.

11. Assume that you have been appointed as CEO of a business unit in a major corporation that has been steadily losing customers, and whose customers have rated it as 'shocking' in terms of service delivery. Identify the aspects that you should consider in terms of trying to instill a service culture in the unit.

Mini Case Study[42]

First Direct was the first bank to offer 24-hour banking directly by telephone, and its service has now been expanded to Internet and cellphone banking. It could be said that it has revolutionised the retail banking industry. The bank realised that people were changing their habits, and would want to bank whenever it suited them. The paradox at First Direct was that it was able to provide better service over the telephone than its competitors could do face to face.

The bank is designed around the customer, focusing on the single customer at the point of contact. It has ensured that all visible signs of structure that would lead to barriers to a good communication with the customer are removed. It works hard in task forces and cross-functional teams to create the culture where things that can create barriers are broken down.

The third aspect that the bank works hard on is spending time and effort on talking about and implementing behaviours that are going to add value to what employees do. For example, all employees undergo six to seven weeks' training before starting work; there is a buddy system and coaching for new recruits; and call centres are measured in terms of customer satisfaction and relationships.

The success of the service culture has resulted in a high number of recommendations by the bank's customers — 33 per cent of customers that join it do so on the basis of a personal recommendation. First Direct believes it should focus on considering the customer's point of view, not the financial point of view, first.

Question

Comment on the service culture of First Direct and indicate how it has achieved superior service throughout the entire bank (make your own assumptions, based on the theoretical background, where necessary).

References

1 Quoted in the *Sunday Times*, 2 October 2005, p. 13.
2 Claycomb, C & Martin, CL. 2002. Building customer relationships: An inventory of service providers' objectives and practices. *Journal of Services Marketing*, 16 (7), pp. 615–20.
3 This section is based on Lamb, CW, Hair, JF & McDaniel, C. 2003. *Essentials of Marketing*. Mason: South-Western, pp. 8–13; Cannon, JP, Perreault, WD & McCarthy, EJ. 2008. *Basic Marketing: A Global-managerial Approach* (16th ed.). New York: McGraw-Hill Irwin, pp. 20–22.
4 Brink, A, Machado, R, Strydom, JW & Cant, MC. 2001. *Customer Relationship Management Principles*. Pretoria: Pinpoint, pp. 16–17.
5 Brink, A & Berndt, A. 2004. *Customer Relationship Management and Customer Service*. Cape Town: Juta, p. 46; Grönroos, C. 2000. *Service Management and Marketing: A Customer Relationship Approach* (2nd ed.). Chichester: Wiley, pp. 98–100.
6 Hoffman, KD & Bateson, JEG. 2006. *Services Marketing, Concepts, Strategies and Cases* (3rd ed.). Mason: Thomson, pp. 320–25.
7 Brink & Berndt, *op. cit.*, p. 70.
8 Claycomb & Martin, *op. cit.*, p. 622.
9 Brink & Berndt, *op. cit.*, p. 70.
10 Adapted from Zeithaml, VA & Bitner, MJ. 2000. *Services Marketing* (2nd ed.). Boston: McGraw-Hill, p. 88.
11 Brink & Berndt, *op. cit.*, pp. 67–69.
12 *Ibid.*, pp. 69–70.
13 Clemmer, J. 2006. Customer/partner (internal and external) focus. <http://www.clemmer.net/articles/subject_4.aspx>, accessed 21 June 2007.
14 Based on Hoffman & Bateson, *op. cit.*, pp. 300–14; Cannon *et al.*, *op. cit.*, pp. 600–2.
15 Parasuraman, A, Zeithaml, VA and Berry, LL. 1988. SERVQUAL: A multiple-item scale for measuring customer perceptions of service quality. *Journal of Retailing*, 64 (1), pp. 12–40.
16 Athanassopoulos, A, Gounaris, S & Stathakopoulos, V. 2001. Behavioural responses to customer satisfaction: An empirical study. *European Journal of Marketing*, 35 (5/6), pp. 687–707.
17 Zeithaml, VA, Bitner, MJ and Gremler, DD. 2006. *Service Quality: Integrating Customer Focus across the Firm.* (4th ed. Boston: McGraw-Hill, p. 154.)
18 Herbst, FJH. 2005. Unpublished course notes, University of Johannesburg.
19 Cronin, JJ and Taylor SA. 1992. Measuring service quality: A reexamination and extension. *Journal of Marketing*, 56 (July), p. 255.

20   Buttle, F. 1996. SERVQUAL: review, critique, research agenda. *European Journal of Marketing*, 30 (1), pp. 8–32.

21   Based on Brink *et al.*, *op. cit.*, pp. 19–21.

22   Brink & Berndt, *op. cit.*, pp. 74–77.

23   *Ibid.*, pp. 75–77.

24   Wikipedia. 2007. Lifetime value. <http://en.wikipedia.org/wiki/Lifetime_value>, accessed 15 August 2007.

25   Harvard Business School Publishing. 2007. Customer lifetime value calculator. <http://harvardbusinessonline.com/flatmm/flashtools/cltv/>, accessed 15 August 2007.

26   Spolsky, J. 2007. Seven steps to remarkable customer service. <http://www.joelonsoftware.com/articles/customerservice.html>, accessed 22 June 2007.

27   Goodman, GS. 2000. *Monitoring, Measuring and Managing Customer Service.* San-Francisco: Jossey-Bass, pp. 4–11, 62, 148–51.

28   Spolsky, *op. cit.*

29   Adapted from Interbrand. 2002. *Uncommon Practice: People Who Deliver a Great Brand Experience.* London: Pearson Education, pp. 90–98.

30   Spolsky, *op. cit.*

31   Goodman, *op. cit.*, pp. 4–11, 62, 148–51.

32   Spolsky, *op. cit.*

33   Goodman, *op. cit.*, pp. 4–11, 62, 148–51.

34   Spolsky, *op. cit.*

35   Goodman, *op. cit.*, pp. 4–11, 62, 148–51.

36   Kim, HW & Kim, YG. 2001. Rationalising the customer service process. *Business Process Management Journal*, pp. 139–56. <http://www.emeraldinsight.com/Insight/viewPDF.jsp?Filename=html/Output/Published/EmeraldFullTextArticle/Pdf/1570070205.pdf>, accessed 21 August 2007.

37   Spolsky, *op. cit.*

38   Brink & Berndt, *op. cit.*, pp. 78–79.

39   Grönroos, *op. cit.*, pp. 98–100.

40   Goodman, *op. cit.*, pp. 4–11, 62, 148–51.

41   *Ibid.*, pp. 152–54.

42   Based on Brink & Berndt, *op. cit.*, pp. 80–81.

CHAPTER 4

Internal Marketing

Learning Outcomes

After studying this chapter, you should be able to:

- define the term 'internal marketing' and the two perspectives associated with internal marketing

- explain the importance of internal marketing to the CRM effort

- explain the five main components of internal marketing and their effect on its overall success

- present a model of internal marketing, using it to explain the key aspects of internal marketing

- explain the integration of the various organisational functions in order to implement a CRM strategy

- explain the different roles carried out by HR management and marketing in the successful implementation of a CRM strategy

- explain the role of trade unions in internal marketing.

4.1   Introduction

One of the key aspects for any organisation implementing CRM is the area of internal marketing. In the chain of relationships, one of the key relationships is found within the organisation itself and is known as internal marketing. The focus of this chapter is what the term 'internal marketing' means and why internal marketing is so important to the successful implementation of CRM within an organisation.

4.2   Definition and Perspectives of Internal Marketing

When talking about internal marketing, there are two groups of people who can be included, namely the internal customers and the employees of the organisation. In the case of internal customers, the organisation can treat them as they would any other customer, making use of marketing strategies to ensure customer satisfaction.

For the purposes of this chapter and the ensuing discussion, internal marketing refers to *the relationship that develops between the employees of the organisation and the organisation itself in order to facilitate the implementation of a CRM programme.* The place of internal marketing is seen in the service triangle illustrated in figure 4.1.

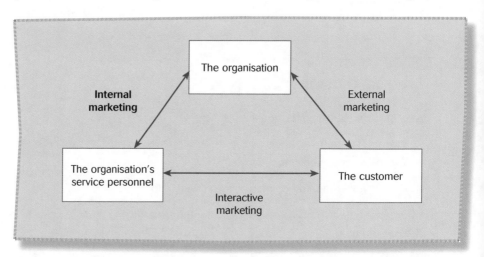

Figure 4.1 The Service Triangle[1]

From this diagram, three types of marketing can be identified, namely interactive marketing (between the service personnel and customers), traditional marketing (between the organisation and customers), and internal marketing between the organisation and the service personnel and other personnel in the organisation. While this diagram identifies service personnel, all employees in an organisation are either themselves interacting with customers or assisting those who are interacting with customers, meaning that *all employees are service personnel in one way or another.*

Definitions of internal marketing identify two dimensions to the concept. The first is the 'marketing job' that the organisation has to do to the staff relating to the job they have, while the second dimension refers to the nature and execution of the task itself. These dimensions and their components are illustrated in figure 4.2.

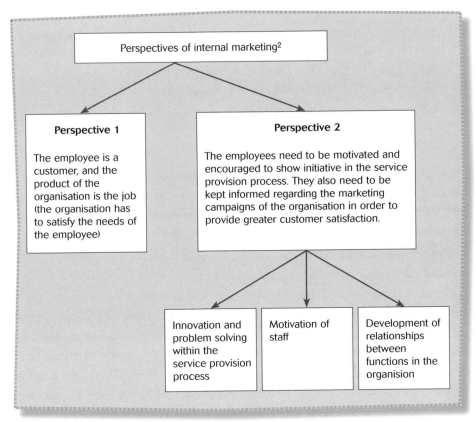

Figure 4.2 The Perspectives of Internal Marketing

4.2.1 Perspective 1

The first perspective of internal marketing relates to the job that is offered to employees. A job can be seen as a 'product' that is offered to an employee.[3] The job and its activities need to be sold (or marketed) in order to attract quality staff, making it a product offered by the organisation. If the product does not satisfy an employee's needs, he/she will find an alternate 'product'.[4] This means that the employee will evaluate the job in terms of its ability to satisfy his/her needs, which refers not only to the financial aspects of the job, but also his/her need for personal growth, as seen in the development and training received from the organisation, as well as the personal development of the employee.

The importance of this perspective is found in the assumption that a satisfied employee will assist in creating satisfied customers for the organisation. The job that a person does within an organisation is hence one that will affect not only the employee him-/herself, but also the success of the organisation.

> When an organisation employs staff, the job description will indicate the nature of the job to be carried out, as well as the remuneration package, and the growth prospects will be discussed with the employee.

4.2.2 Perspective 2

A number of definitions of internal marketing have been offered to identify the nature of the second dimension of internal marketing, namely the nature and execution of the marketing task. Each of these definitions attempts to put the focus on a different aspect that forms part of this perspective.

The first aspect refers to the activities of the tasks that are needed to ensure that the external marketing is carried out successfully. This can be seen in the following definition: 'Internal marketing is any form of marketing within an organisation that focuses staff attention on the internal activities that need to be changed in order to enhance external marketplace performance.'[5] The focus here is on the purpose that can be identified for internal marketing, namely that of the channelling of staff commitment into the activities of the organisation. This staff commitment is channelled specifically into the issues of problem solving and opportunity seeking within the marketing efforts in order to improve customer service. This would imply that without employees who are focused on solving the problems experienced by external markets, the success of the marketing effort will be compromised. An example of this may be the situation where employees are encouraged to show initiative and develop new methods of improving customer care, where they see the opportunity. This might involve new processing techniques or the introduction of new production methods.

> Suppose a salesperson in a motor vehicle dealership sees an opportunity to improve his and the dealership's level of customer service, he should have the freedom to be able to bring about the necessary changes, e.g. offering after-hours test drives of motor vehicles, or the delivery of a vehicle to an interested customer for a test drive.

Linked to the above is the second aspect, namely that of the human resource issues within the organisation, specifically that of motivation: 'Internal marketing is a planned effort using a marketing-like approach directed at motivating employees, for implementing and integrating organisational strategies towards customer orientation.[6] In this definition, the question of the motivation of staff to attain the goals set for the CRM programme can be seen. Here the focus of marketing activities is the employees, where the purpose of internal marketing is to get the staff motivated so that they are willing and able to implement all the strategies of the organisation, including CRM and other strategies of the marketing department. In attempting to motivate staff, attention is drawn to the issues such as performance-based reward systems, training and other techniques that can be used to affect the motivation of the workforce. This can be done by linking staff bonuses to their success in retaining profitable customers for the organisation.

> The CRM programme contains a number of objectives that are to be attained. Goals need to be set that are regarded as challenging for the employees, and for which they will be adequately rewarded.

The third aspect highlighted by internal marketing is the relationships that are created as a result of internal marketing: 'The objective of internal marketing is to create relationships between management, employees and the various functions within the organisation.[7] No function can exist in isolation, hence the aim of internal marketing efforts is to create an efficient unit, where functions are all focused on achieving a common goal. This is done through the creation of relationships among the various functions of the organisation. These relationships are not only created through formal contacts and communication within the organisation, but also through informal contacts such as social events and get-togethers.

> If a customisation programme is to be implemented as part of a CRM strategy, it will mean that each function will have to adapt accordingly. This will mean, for example, that purchasing will change the items purchased (both in volume and specification), while continuing to affect the other components of the value chain.

From the above definitions, a number of key aspects can be identified:

- No CRM strategy can be successfully implemented without the support of the people (staff) in the employ of the organisation.

- The attitudes and motivation of staff have a direct impact on the service offered to customers.

- Organisations should seek to have motivated employees who are able to deliver superior levels of service to the external customers.

- Staff do not work in isolation, but all organisational functions are required to work together to maximise the benefits of the CRM strategy within the organisation.

Incorporating the above perspectives, internal marketing can be defined as a *'planned effort using a marketing-like approach directed at motivating employees, for implementing and integrating organisational strategies towards customer orientation'*.[8]

4.3 The Importance of Internal Marketing in CRM

The importance of internal marketing can be seen in the two perspectives identified above. If employees do not believe that their needs (both financial and personal) are being satisfied, they will find another employer who will satisfy these needs. This means that internal marketing has an effect on staff turnover and retention levels, as a satisfied staff member of staff is more likely to stay in the employ of the organisation.[9]

Further, the importance of internal marketing is seen in how it affects the organisation and its performance. This is based on the assumption that there is a link between the satisfaction of employees and the customer satisfaction delivered by an organisation — what is known as the 'happy staff equals happy customer' logic.[10] This will imply that the marketing activities of the organisation will be performed effectively, as the staff are being treated the way that they would want customers to be treated.

There is also the effect that internal marketing has on the external market, such as customers and suppliers. Customer retention involves keeping customers in the long term, which can be an objective of a CRM strategy. Customer retention can be traced to the relationship that the customer has with an employee that has been built up over time. It has been suggested that many customers are more loyal to a particular employee than they are to the organisation itself.[11] The loss of his/her personal relationship with an employee can be cited as a reason why a customer will follow an employee to a new employer.[12] Examples of this are seen in the case of hairdressers and doctors. Internal marketing can affect suppliers in that motivated staff will seek to build relationships with suppliers, to the benefit of the organisation. They will also deliver superior service to these suppliers, thus benefitting the organisation.

Hence, both the individual and the organisation will benefit from internal marketing, as will the external customer, who is receiving superior service from the organisation as a whole, and from the employee.

4.4 The Components of Internal Marketing

Taking the perspectives of internal marketing into account, five main components can be identified.[13] These components are regarded as essential in the implementation of a successful internal marketing programme. They are as follows:

- **Employee motivation and satisfaction:** Here the focus is on the people in the employ of the organisation and the skills that they have, as well as their motivation to provide the expected level of service. If the motivation of employees is not adequate, it will affect the levels of service offered, which in turn will impact on the satisfaction experienced by customers.

- **Customer orientation and customer service:** Here the focus of the organisation is on the customer, in contrast to having a sales focus. This results in employees being customer aware in the activities that they carry out. Customer satisfaction is the key to maintaining customers and their support of the organisation.

- **Interfunctional co-ordination and integration:** The importance of co-operation among all the functions is identified. No function can operate in isolation, and the success of the entire programme requires that every function needs the other to operate efficiently.

- **Marketing-like approach to the components above:** This approach suggests the use of marketing-like techniques within the organisation. These marketing-like techniques can be used to inform employees about the actions and decisions of the organi-sation regarding marketing activities. Examples include the use of marketing communication within the organisation and other promotional activities.

- **Implementation of specific corporate or functional strategies:** Staff are the keys to the implementation of any strategy within the organisation. Any CRM strategy needs communication and co-operation within the organisation to aid in its implementation. Internal marketing can thus be used to assist in strategy implementation, while also improving interfunctional co-operation within the organisation.

4.5 A Model of Internal Marketing

A variety of models of internal marketing have been proposed, reflecting the various perspectives of internal marketing. The model illustrated in figure 4.3 attempts to combine both the perspectives of internal marketing as discussed earlier, as well as the components discussed above, in order to integrate them.

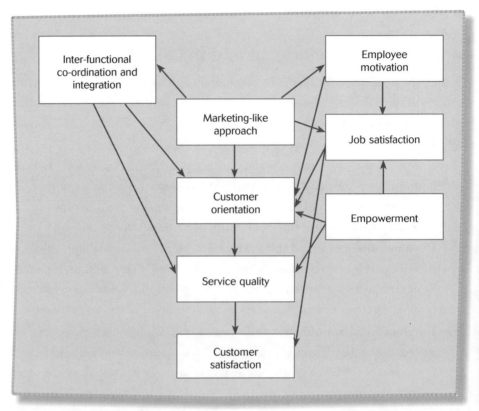

Figure 4.3 A Model of Internal Marketing[14]

The desired outcome according to this model is that of customer satisfaction. This end result is affected not only by the human resources issues (the right-hand side of figure 4.3), but also by the marketing activities within the organisation.

There are a number of components to the model that need further discussion:

- **Marketing-like approach:** This approach seeks to affect not only the way in which the organisation's external customers are treated, but also the way in which its functions interact with one another. Communication regarding marketing and other activities can also impact on the employees' motivation and the satisfaction they derive from their jobs. This marketing approach results in a customer orientation for the organisation.

- **Customer orientation:** This serves as the key to satisfied customers. The customer orientation has an impact on the service quality that is offered to final consumers, while also affecting the organisation as a whole. This customer orientation means that the customer is the focus of the attention of all activities in the organisation. This customer orientation is derived from the marketing-like approach that is adopted by the organisation, and is made possible through the empowerment of staff and the co-operation of all the functions in the organisation.

- **Service quality:** This refers to the customer's overall perception of the relative inferiority/superiority of the organisation and its services.[15] The service quality is not only determined by the job satisfaction experienced by employees, but there are also a number of other factors that can contribute.

- **Customer satisfaction:** The focus of all the components is the satisfaction of customer needs. Satisfaction is seen as the ongoing evaluation of an organisation's ability to deliver the benefits that a customer is seeking.[16] Job satisfaction and service quality have a direct effect on customer satisfaction, while the other factors play an indirect role in the satisfaction experienced. A satisfied customer will tend to do business with the organisation again and again, to the advantage of the organisation.

- **Interfunctional co-ordination and integration:** A marketing-like approach affects the co-operation that takes place among the various functions. The interaction that takes place among the functions will affect the customer orientation seen in the behaviour of staff, while also affecting the service quality received by the final consumers.

- **Employee motivation:** Motivation takes place through the marketing-like approach used within the organisation. This motivation will in turn affect the job satisfaction and the customer orientation of the employee.

- **Empowerment:** This refers to the initiative that the employees can show in their job situation, and this can result in the employees doing what they think is necessary to satisfy the customer's needs. Certain guidelines can be laid down within which employees are free to operate. Empowerment affects the job satisfaction experienced, the customer orientation of the employees and the service quality received in the purchase situation.

- **Job satisfaction:** The impact of job satisfaction on customer satisfaction is seen indirectly through the customer orientation that exists in the organisation. This refers back to the assumed link between the satisfaction of employees and the customer satisfaction delivered by the organisation. Job satisfaction is affected by the marketing-like approach used within the organisation, as well as the degree of empowerment that an individual employee has in the work situation. In turn, this job satisfaction can be seen in the customer orientation displayed by employees when providing service to customers.

4.6   Interfunctional Co-ordination and Integration

The issue that requires further investigation is the question of the exact nature of the interaction that is required among the functions of the organisation. As mentioned earlier, it is necessary that the various functions are co-ordinated and integrated, and it is necessary to examine the nature of this interaction. It implies that the functions affect one another, but also that they work together towards attaining the goal and mission of the organisation and attaining success in the CRM strategy.

The functions discussed below are those that are generally found in organisations. While they may not be exactly the same in all organisations, the general principles are still applicable within the functions of any organisation. A further reason for the examination of the various functions is to illustrate clearly the role that they fulfil in the CRM process, and to show the importance of CRM to each function.

Questions may be asked by the various functions of the organisation concerning the costs associated with CRM, as well as the capability of the organisation to implement the strategy successfully. It is these issues that need to be addressed with each function. Without commitment from all the functions involved, CRM implementation will be hampered, affecting the organisation as a whole.

4.6.1   The Financial Function

The financial function has the task of managing the organisation's financial resources. The questions that may be asked by those in the financial function include the following:

- What are the costs associated with any CRM strategy?
- What are the time costs that will be associated with implementing CRM?
- What will the additional income be as a result of the implementation of a CRM strategy by the organisation?
- Will a CRM strategy create value for the shareholders?

These questions need to be adequately dealt with if the support of the financial function is to be obtained. What causes concern for the financial function is the additional costs associated with any CRM programme. These costs include the costs of the technology and training required for CRM. These costs should be put into the context of the additional income and subsequent profits associated with the CRM programme. The important fact that has to be borne in mind is that any CRM programme does not yield short-term benefits; rather, it has a long-term effect. This implies that money may be invested without an immediate direct return.

The Value-Driver model can be used to determine the total market value of the organisation rather than using accounting-based methods such as earnings per share and traditional ratio analysis.[17] Furthermore, additional value can be obtained from existing customers. This additional value can be derived from a reduction in the costs associated with each customer, the reduced time taken to market the product to the customer and the lessened business risk associated with the customer.[18]

Share value will be affected, as current customers can be made more profitable, while those that are not regarded as profitable will be removed from the organisation's portfolio.[19] Furthermore, CRM can indicate growth opportunities for the organisation, as new products can be better tested and marketed in the marketplace.

4.6.2 Human Resource (HR) Management

From a closer examination of the two perspectives of internal marketing, the perception may exists that internal marketing is merely a dimension of HR management and, as such, forms part of the HR function within the organisation. The references earlier to the issues of motivation and human resources as aspects of internal marketing may tend to show internal marketing to be another dimension of the HR function, which is a view held by some.[20]

The task of the HR practitioner in the organisation is the recruitment of human resources for the organisation, and the training, development and maintenance of these resources.[21] This means that the recruitment, selection, placement and induction of staff remains the task of the HR function within the organisation. The dividing line between the HR function and the internal marketing process is found in the nature of the authority that is used in its implementation. The use of formal authority (or force) does not form part of internal marketing; rather, it forms part of the techniques that can be used by the HR function to ensure compliance with a particular course of action.[22] It is essential that policies be developed by the HR

Assume that a local bank is attempting to improve customer service through a CRM programme. This will require internal marketing within the organisation, but if there are not enough staff to do the job, the CRM programme will not be successful. It will be the task of the HR function to employ additional suitable staff with the correct qualifications and skills. It will also be the task of the HR function to carry out the necessary induction and other training programmes. It will be the task of the marketing function to implement aspects specific to the CRM programme. Co-operation will be needed to ensure that policies and performance schemes support the CRM programme.

function that are supportive of the internal marketing activities and contribute to the corporate climate that exists within the organisation. Decisions regarding motivation and performance reward systems also form part of the link between the HR department and the marketing department, making this interaction vital.

4.6.3 The Information Technology Function

Many regard information as the key to a successful CRM strategy. A CRM strategy requires both hardware and software that an organisation may not have, which contributes to the overall costs of the strategy. Decisions have to be made concerning the appropriate software and the way in which it will be used in the CRM strategy. As the CRM strategy progresses, the requirements of a particular function may change, and integration is required to ensure that the necessary changes are made. Various software programmes can be developed or purchased that will suit the needs of the organisation, and these needs have to be constantly monitored, as well as the suitability of the programme to the long-term needs of the organisation. The use of data mining will also have to be decided upon, as well as the programmes that will be used.

While information concerning consumers may be crucial to the success of CRM, information concerning staff is also useful in the internal marketing campaign. The information that the HR function has at its disposal about staff can be used as a basis for segmenting the staff and so determining the nature and quantity of the information that will be given to the various staff members about the CRM strategy.[23]

4.6.4 Operations Management

Operations management is the function in the organisation that is responsible for the actual manufacture of the product for sale to final consumers.[24] The information that is collected as part of the CRM strategy needs to be fed through to this function in order to make product adaptations as required by customers, especially if there is a high degree of customisation.

One of the aspects affecting the operations function specifically is the issue of Total Quality Management (TQM) and its implementation within the organisation. As a philosophy, TQM is a corporate strategy that focuses on obtaining customer satisfaction through the delivery of superior-quality products.[25] There are three basic principles that form the basis of this philosophy, namely:

- the empowerment of employees;
- the continuous improvement of quality; and
- the use of quality improvement teams.

As a result of these principles, the product offered is one that has been carefully designed and one that can be produced consistently. Many organisations are finding a link among the quality of the product as it forms part of the TQM strategy, employee satisfaction and customer satisfaction.[26] Internal marketing thus serves as the link between the quality of the product and the satisfaction of the external customer. As customer satisfaction is the focus of the organisation, TQM can play an important role in this process. This process can be illustrated in the virtuous cycle of internal marketing in figure 4.4.

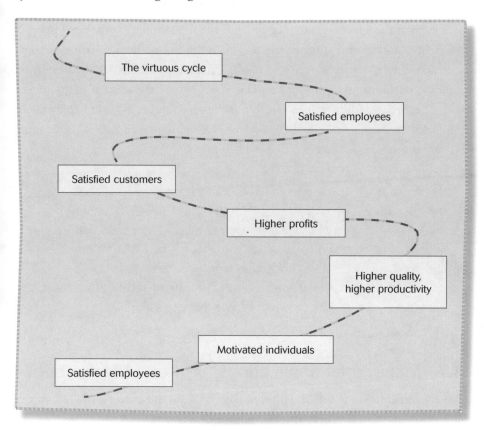

The virtuous cycle

Satisfied employees

Satisfied customers

Higher profits

Higher quality, higher productivity

Motivated individuals

Satisfied employees

Figure 4.4 The Virtuous Cycle of Internal Marketing[27]

4.6.5 Corporate Communication/Public Relations

The public relations function manages the image of the organisation among groups and individuals outside the organisation, such as the government, members of the community at large and trade unions.[28] Bringing about changes within the organisation may have an effect on these groups' perceptions of the organisation, and it may require this function to manage this process.

Using a strategy of disciplining or firing of employees as part of a CRM strategy may create a negative image in the community regarding the organisation. Under these circumstances, public relations can explain the reasons for the actions and seek to minimise the negative publicity associated with these actions.

4.6.6 Inbound Logistics (Purchasing)

The focus of this function is the acquiring of the right product at the right price, in the right quantities and at the right time.[29] It is the task of the purchasing manager to ensure that adequate supplies of raw materials are obtained at the best price. Building relationships with suppliers also forms part of the purchasing manager's task. These relationships will be valuable as the organisation begins to apply CRM principles, as this may require different levels of supply, or a change in the re-order quantities of the various stock items.

Suppose a motor vehicle manufacturer begins to customise products to satisfy the specific needs of its customers. This requires different items to be kept in stock, and at different stock levels. The rate at which specific stock items are used may also change. This may mean that smaller amounts of, for example, leather will be kept in stock, while more fabric of different designs will be required. It may also require special sourcing of items to meet specific customer needs, such as leather or fabric of a specific type or colour.

4.7 Managerial Implications of Internal Marketing

The implementation of CRM within the organisation will have a profound impact on management styles and the decisions that are made. As indicated earlier, empowerment of staff is needed to improve the customer satisfaction offered. This requires a specific style of management, with which the managers may not currently be familiar. It also requires changes in the corporate culture of the organisation, as well as increasing the levels of responsibility of particular managers. Further, this requires that managers trust their employees, and show this trust in the way in which their employees are managed. This trust needs to be mutual in nature, and without this trust, performance and communication will be adversely affected. This will be discussed in more detail under the implementation issues of CRM strategies.

Communication with employees remains critical in building relationships with employees, and hence the important role of various communication tools such as the Intranet, newsletters and circulars.

4.8   The Roles of Employees in Internal Marketing

Not all staff are equally involved with customers, and therefore different staff members have different effects on customers. Four categories of employees can be identified, each having a different role to play in reaching customers.[30]

- **Contactors:** These are employees who are highly involved in customer contact. They tend to occupy selling and customer-service positions within the organisation. This means they have direct contact with customers that requires knowledge of the organisation and its products, as they are involved with the traditional marketing activities of the organisation. This requires customer-oriented people who can deal with situations presented to them, and this tends to serve as the basis for their salaries.

- **Modifiers:** These are people who have indirect contact with customers, as they are not involved in traditional marketing activities. They include accounting staff, as well as security personnel and receptionists.

- **Influencers:** They are involved with the traditional elements of the marketing mix, but they have no customer contact. Their activities should nonetheless respond to the needs of customers, and examples include market researchers and product development specialists.

- **Isolateds:** These are people who have little, if any, client contact and who are not involved in marketing activities. Their tasks include purchasing and warehousing, as well as information-processing activities.

4.9   Trade Unions and Internal Marketing

Trade unions play an important role in an organisation, as they have the task of communicating the views of workers to management.[31] As a result of this, the organisation may change its way of operating or doing business. Building a relationship with the unions is critical, as it is through them that the organisation can communicate with employees. Building a good relationship with the unions can also affect decisions regarding strike action, which is one of the tools used by unions.[32] Obviously, a strike is not good for any party (neither the organisation nor the workers, as both lose money). Furthermore, once a strike is over, the organisation and the unions will have to start rebuilding their relationship.

4.10 Tools in Implementing Internal Marketing

Two perspectives can be used in identifying the tasks involved in implementing internal marketing. One perspective suggests using the marketing mix and directing it inward.[33] This would indicate that each element of the marketing mix would be used to communicate with employees as to the exact nature of the marketing activities involved, as well as their contribution to these activities. This ensures that employees are aware of the marketing activities of the organisation. It is also necessary for the organisation to ensure that employees are motivated, and so internal communication techniques are required to keep everyone informed regarding any developments in the organisation. Other tools that can be used in internal marketing include training and motivation. Training will enable employees to become familiar with the activities associated with their jobs, making them more efficient and more productive, which in turn affects their motivational level.

> Motivation of staff is an area about which much has been written. Wesbank has developed a number of strategies that are used to encourage its staff in their work, not only to benefit themselves, but also to give something back to the community. In 2002, Wesbank reached its target of providing R2 billion in vehicle financing. To mark this achievement, staff were given a choice of receiving a DVD player or a VCR. Together with parties to celebrate the event, the cost to Wesbank amounted to R7 million.[34]

Further strategies include improving organisational communication and increasing the level of bonding between the organisation and the employees, by making them feel connected to the organisation and committed to its values and mission.

4.11 Summary

The focus of this chapter has been on the issues affecting and the importance of internal marketing in the area of CRM, and how organisations go about building relationships with their employees. The chapter started by examining the perspectives that comprise internal marketing, which are reflected in the model of internal marketing. Functional co-ordination and co-operation are essential to the success of a CRM programme, and the chapter examined the various functions and how their interactions affect one another. It concluded with a discussion of the roles that employees can play within the organisation, and how internal marketing can take place.

Discussion Questions

1. Explain the term 'internal marketing'.
2. Explain the two perspectives that make up the concept of internal marketing.
3. Explain the model of internal marketing, using it to indicate the two perspectives of internal marketing.
4. 'HR management and internal marketing are really the same thing.' Comment on this statement, indicating whether you agree with it or not. Motivate your answer.
5. Explain how the functions of an organisation interact to implement a CRM strategy.
6. Explain four roles that staff can play within an organisation according to the degree of customer contact they have.
7. Explain three tools that managers can use to implement an internal marketing strategy.

Mini Case Study[35, 36]

The South African banking and financial services sector is regarded by many as one of the most sophisticated in the world. The various banks seek to satisfy the needs of the various sectors in the South African population. The needs of these sectors range from the most basic customers who require a bank account in order to access their salary cheques, to those who are very wealthy. It is particularly the last sector that many of the banks target, since they believe that high profits can be made from these clients.

This is a very competitive market, with a great deal of effort being expended by a bank such as Investec Private Bank, as well as a range of other international banks, to attract these high-wealth clients to the bank.

Investec Private Bank has three components, each trying to reach a separate segment of the market. Investec's international bank offers services to clients who have R10 million worth of bankable assets and R50 million net asset value. They are regarded as internationally wealthy and are catered for through Investec's international network. Less affluent clients are catered for in the bank's private client division and in its professional banking arm.

These wealthy clients have money to invest and large assets. They focus their needs on obtaining an excellent return on their investments, as well as receiving excellent service. They also want access to their money anywhere, anytime, as they tend to be a very mobile group.

To satisfy the needs of this select group, banks have individual consultants known as private bankers whose task it is to build a relationship with each of their clients. Private bankers have access to the bank's database in order to collect information on their clients so as to better satisfy their needs. This means that a private banker can take the initiative in developing investment and banking packages uniquely tailored to the needs of a specific person.

Products offered include credit cards and home loans, as well as investment products such as private money funds and stockbroking.

Questions

1. Explain how Investec Private Bank provides customer satisfaction in its service provision process.

2. Explain how empowerment can assist in improving the employee satisfaction levels within Investec Private Bank.

3. Assume that Investec has decided to expand the range of services it offers to international bank clients. How would this affect the financial function within the bank?

4. What internal marketing tools would Investec Private Bank use to increase employee satisfaction?

References

1   Parasuraman, A. 2000. Technology Readiness Index (TRI): A multiple-item scale to measure readiness to embrace new technologies. *Journal of Service Research*, 2 (4), p. 308.

2   Ahmed, PK & Rafiq, M. 2002. *Internal Marketing: Tools and Concepts for Customer-focused Management*. Oxford: Butterworth-Heinemann, pp. 13–15.

3   Ballantyne, D. 2000. Internal relationship marketing: A strategy for knowledge renewal. *International Journal of Bank Marketing*, 18 (6), p. 276.

4   Ahmed & Rafiq, *op. cit.*, p. 28.

5   Ballantyne, D, Christopher, M & Payne, A. 1995. Improving the quality of services marketing: (Re)design is the critical link. *Journal of Marketing Management*, 2 (1), p. 15.

6   Ahmed & Rafiq, *op. cit.*, p. 11.

7   Gummesson, E. 2002. *Total Relationship Marketing (2nd ed.)*. Oxford: Butterworth-Heinemann, p. 198.

8   Ahmed & Rafiq, *op. cit.*, p. 11.

9   Payne, A, Christopher, M, Clark, M & Peck, H. 1995. *Relationship Marketing for Competitive Advantage.* Oxford: Butterworth-Heinemann, p. 12.

10 *Ibid.*, p. 276.

11 *Ibid.*, p. 12.

12 Du Plessis, PJ, Jooste, CJ & Strydom, JW. 2001. *Applied Strategic Marketing.* Sandown: Heinemann, p. 88.

13 Ahmed & Rafiq, *op. cit.*, p. 9.

14 *Ibid.*, p. 20.

15 Green, S. & Boshoff, C. 2002. An empirical assessment of the relationships between service quality, satisfaction and value: A tourism study. *Management Dynamics*, 11 (3), p. 4.

16 *Ibid.*, p. 3.

17 Gordon, IH. 1998. *Relationship Marketing.* Toronto: John Wiley, p. 88.

18 *Ibid.*, p. 89.

19 *Ibid.*, p. 90.

20 Ballantyne, *op. cit.*, p. 276.

21 Cronje, GJ de J., Du Toit, GS & Motlana, MDC. 2000. *Introduction to Business Management* (5th ed.). Oxford: Oxford University Press, p. 440.

22 Ahmed & Rafiq, *op. cit.*, p. 60.

23 *Ibid.*, p. 39.

24 Nieman, G & Bennett, A. 2000. *Business Management: A Value Chain Approach.* Pretoria: Van Schaik, p. 153.

25 Ahmed & Rafiq, *op. cit.*, p. 94.

26 *Ibid.*, p. 111.

27 *Ibid.*, p. 110.

28 Nieman & Bennett, *op. cit.*, p. 243.

29 *Ibid.*, p. 396.

30 Du Plessis *et al.*, *op. cit.*, p. 272.

31 Noe, RA, Hollenbeck, JR, Gerhardt, B & Wright, PM. 2000. *Human Resources Management: Gaining a Competitive Advantage* (3rd ed.). Boston: Irwin McGraw-Hill, p. 493.

32 *Ibid.*

33 Ballantyne, *op. cit.*, p. 276.

34 Furlonger, D. 2002. Motoring to the next milestone. *Financial Mail*, 1 November. <http://secure.financialmail.co.za/02/1101/cover/coverstoryd.html>, accessed 28 January 2003.

35 Wood, S. 2002. House calls. *Financial Mail.* <http://secure.financialmail.co.za/99/0618/personal/apriv.html>, accessed 7 January 2003.

36 Wood, S. 2002. Identity crisis: Investing for wealthy individuals. *Financial Mail.* <http://secure.financialmail.co.za/report/privatebank/apb.html>, accessed 7 January 2003.

One-to-One Marketing and Mass Customisation

Learning Outcomes

After studying this chapter, you should be able to:

- explain the term one-to-one (1:1) marketing and differentiate it from traditional marketing

- explain the advantages of 1:1 marketing for the organisation

- explain the steps in the 1:1 marketing process

- define the term customisation and differentiate mass customisation from personalisation

- explain the preconditions needed for mass customisation

- explain three approaches to customisation.

A. 1:1 MARKETING

5.1 Introduction

There are two parts to the chapter, namely the one dealing with 1:1 marketing and the one dealing with mass customisation. This marketing approach seeks to identify individual consumers of a product, while mass customisation seeks to adapt products and production to meet the specific needs of these identified customers. The first step in creating successful customer relationships involves establishing a 1:1 relationship, after which the second step of mass customisation follows.[1] These two steps are regarded as inseparable, and both are needed to derive the full benefit from customer relationship management.

5.2 Definition of 1:1 Marketing

One-to-one marketing works on the principle of marketing to and targeting a customer individually. Traditionally, the concept of marketing has revolved around selling as many products to as many customers as possible. The use of market segmentation made it possible to sell a single standard product to as many customers as possible. 1:1 marketing seeks to sell that one specific customer as many products as possible over a period of time and across different product lines.[2] This requires a change in mindset in that the focus is not the number of customers that the organisation seeks to reach with the product; rather, it is the number of products that each individual customer buys that counts. This is known as the *share of customer* (as contrasted with market share in traditional marketing). Hence, 1:1 marketing does not mean interacting on a 1:1 basis with every customer, but rather evaluating each customer and determining a marketing strategy based on the profitability of the group or customer.[3]

If a florist shop (or other retailer) advertises, it is able to increase the number of products sold. Suppose, however, a florist sends a postcard to customers reminding them of a number of different aspects: 1) that a special event is coming up soon; 2) what flowers each customer sent on this occasion the previous year; and 3) that a telephone call to a specific number will get flowers delivered this year. This would indicate that the florist has a record of all transactions and that it wants to keep the business of its existing customers. It does not mean that new customers are not important; it is, rather, encouraging existing customers to use the service again.[4]

5.3 Contrasting 1:1 Marketing with Mass Marketing

Mass marketing is the marketing that has traditionally taken place where the market consists of people who are relatively similar (i.e. who are in the same market segment) and who are exposed to high levels of advertising.[5]

Table 5.1 Contrasting Mass Marketing and 1:1 Marketing[6]

Mass marketing	1:1 marketing
Product managers seek to maximise the sales of their product i.e. to as many customers as possible	Customer managers seek to sell as many products as possible to one customer at a time
New customers are sought on a continual basis	New business from current customers is also sought
Economies of *scale* is the focus	Economies of *scope* is the focus. (This refers to the extent of the knowledge that the organisation has concerning a customer, where the more information an organisation has, the better the quality of the relationship with the customer.[7])

5.4 Advantages/Benefits of 1:1 Marketing

There are a number of advantages that can be gained from the use of 1:1 marketing by an organisation.

- **The ability to track defections by customers:** In the case of mass products, the manufacturer of a breakfast cereal knows the sales levels in a specific geographical area, but does not know how these fit together or the specific details of each sale. If a customer does not purchase the product for a specific reason, there is no way the organisation can keep track of this information. It is only through 1:1 marketing that the organisation can track defections and attempt to find the reason for these defections.[8]

- **The ability to know customers more deeply and so able to satisfy needs more adequately:** Information concerning the customer can be collected and used to develop products and services that satisfy the needs of the customer better.

5.5   The Steps in the 1:1 Marketing Process

A number of steps make up the 1:1 marketing process.[9]

 Step 1: Identify individual customers and establish how they can be reached

It must be possible for the organisation not only to identify its customers, but to specifically identify its valuable customers. In identifying these valuable customers, it is necessary to have a great deal of information about these customers. It is not enough to have their ages, income and other demographic criteria; rather, database management needs to be used in order to collect detailed information. This would include a record of customers' purchasing behaviour as well as their preferences over a period of time. It may require the co-operation of customers to make this information available, as required by the learning relationship.

 Step 2: Differentiate customers by their needs and values

In order to make the 1:1 experience meaningful, it is necessary that customers can be differentiated according to their needs and the values that make them unique from each other. The differentiation will indicate the most suitable and appropriate strategies that can be used to reach them with the organisation's product. The strategies selected will be derived from the information that has been collected about customers' habits and preferences. (If it is not possible to differentiate customers, then the need for 1:1 marketing and mass customisation should be questioned.)

 Step 3: Interact with customers to establish a dialogue

Creating customer dialogue is a vital part of building customer relationships. Without dialogue, no relationship can develop or flourish. The organisation has to determine the best ways of establishing customer contact in order to develop a meaningful dialogue with its customers. Organisations have traditionally advertised their product in the media or sent customers letters in the mail, seeing these methods as ways of developing dialogue. Unfortunately for the organisation, customers do not perceive this as being a way of creating dialogue. The way that customers have been able to communicate has been through the use of toll-free numbers, as well as writing letters. While this has proved useful to the organisation, this also does not constitute dialogue.[10] Club card schemes can be useful in creating the forum for dialogue to take place, but in many cases they are used to sell products, thus not creating dialogue in the process.

To create dialogue, it is necessary that customers and the organisation are prepared to exchange views about much more than just customers' purchasing activities. This requires a high degree of participation and commitment from both parties.

> Suppose a customer were to call in to a toll-free number of a large organisation. This could create the opportunity to exchange views and ask questions about the product's features, like its variations, sizes and packaging. This could be done by asking the customer a number of questions in the course of the phone call.[11]

One of the ways of increasing the dialogue is to make use of technology, such as the Internet, websites, voice mail and SMSs.

Step 4: Customise the organisation's products

Once customers have informed you about their perceived needs, it is necessary to ensure that you have a product that can meet these needs. This forms part of the mass customisation process that your organisation has developed. It may involve customising the product or the service itself. Without this customisation process, the information that has been gathered is of no use, and is not being adequately exploited.

Step 5: Make the relationship a continuous learning relationship

This step focuses on the long-term building that that takes place with respect to the relationship. Relationships are not static, and as such require continual inputs from both parties if they are to be regarded as mutually beneficial. (The learning relationship is discussed in detail later in the chapter. It was also dealt with in chapter 2.)

Once having created a 1:1 organisation with a 1:1 view of each customer, it is necessary for the organisation to ensure that the products offered are customised to meet the needs of its various types of customers.

B. MASS CUSTOMISATION

Mass customisation is the second critical decision in CRM, and is also a decision that affects the entire organisation. Customisation does not only refer to the customisation of products, but also the customisation of services.

5.6 Definition of Mass Customisation

Mass customisation can be defined as *'the process of providing and supporting profitably individually tailored goods and services, according to each customer's preferences with regard to form, time, place and price'*.[12] From this definition, a number of comments can be made about what customisation means to the organisation.

- **Providing and supporting:** It is not enough to provide only the customised product or service, but it is also necessary to provide adequate support to the customisation process in order to keep customers' needs satisfied, and to ensure that customisation is successful in the long term. This would require the provision of after-sales service and a warrantee/guarantee service.

- **Profitable:** Without the profits that can accrue from implementing customisation, there is no point in continuing with it. This implies that the customers should not be offered an unlimited number of options of products and services, as this would not be profitable for the organisation.[13] Therefore, the organisation should not consider offering certain options.

- **Individually tailored:** Customisation implies that products are designed individually to suit a market of one.[14] This means that the product is designed specifically to satisfy individual needs that have been identified as part of the 1:1 process.

- **Goods and services:** Both goods and services can be customised. Products such as motor vehicles and clothing can be customised to suit the requirements of the customer, while in the case of a leasing or financial service, for example, adjustments can be made to suit the needs of the customer.

- **Customer preferences:** These preferences must be unique so that the organisation is able to develop a product that can satisfy these preferences. If needs are too similar, it may not be profitable to customise any of the product line.

- **Form, time, place and price:** Customer needs should differ as to the nature of the desired product, when the product is required and the price the customer is prepared to pay for the product. The customisation process has to allow this to take place.

A further definition can be given that places the concept in a slightly different light. Mass customisation can further be regarded as *the use of flexible processes and organisational structures to produce varied and often customised products and services at the low cost of a standardised, mass-production system*.[15] The goal of this process is to create a range of products and product options from which the customer can select, and to customise a product from within the range. Mass customisation should provide the benefits of the mass-production system with the benefits of individualised need satisfaction.

> Levi Strauss makes use of customisation in the sale of its jeans. Customers can have their measurements taken in one of 56 stores, and these measurements are stored on record. The jeans are manufactured specially for the client to fit the measurements. These jeans retail at a premium of 20 per cent more than the cost of the mass-manufactured product.[16]

Mass customisation can also be differentiated from customisation. Customisation is when one product is adapted and delivered to a customer, while mass customisation is when the customisation of products becomes routine for the organisation.[17]

5.7 Customisation and Personalisation

It is further necessary to differentiate customisation from personalisation. Personalisation is defined as *'the process that enables communication, products and services to bear the name of the customer, [thus] adding value to the customer as they position themselves with others'*.[18] Examples of personalisation include putting a customer's name on diaries, caps and clothing, as well as on communications such as on letters sent to the customer. Having a name on a letter or on an item does not mean that the personalisation is worth a great deal to the customer. For personalisation to be favourably perceived by the customer, it has to have value. This means that some personalisation is more valuable than others, depending on the perceptions and expectations of a particular customer.

> An example of personalisation is the letters we receive that attempt to sell us roofing, or painting or a variety of household services. We ignore and discard many of these letters, as they do not have value for us as customers. They are personal, but they are not personalised.

If personalisation is to have a high degree of value to the organisation and, by implication, to the customer, it needs to be combined with customisation.[19] In that way, the customer is prepared to pay for the additional value that has been created specifically to satisfy his/her unique needs.

5.8 Preconditions for Mass Customisation[20]

It is clear that customisation is an area that requires decisions to be made by the organisation. Not all products can be customised to the same extent. Before embarking on customisation within the organisation, care needs to be taken that this is the correct step for the organisation to take. Thus the organisation needs to answer the question: Should we be customising the product? In order to do that, a number of preconditions need to be examined.

5.8.1 Individual Needs and Preferences

In many instances, it would appear that customer needs are the same, but closer examination will indicate that these needs are, in fact, different. Without there being a significant difference between the needs of people, customisation is not needed. As people's need differ, so they will require a product that differs, albeit slightly, to satisfy their different needs. This requires a great deal of research on the part of the organisation to ensure that the nature of the differences in the needs has been determined and that these needs can be profitably satisfied.

5.8.2 Assembling Unique Offerings

It must be possible for the organisation to develop a unique product offering, and for this to be offered to the customer. If the organisation is unable to manufacture this product, it cannot be offered in the marketplace. Another option is that the customer can assemble the unique product, if this cannot be done by the organisation.

> IKEA provides furniture that customers can assemble, once they have selected the components that they would like. This gives the individual customer the freedom to select only the components he/she wants, thereby satisfying his/her unique needs.

5.8.3 Customer Appreciation

Customisation has to satisfy the needs of customers, and they will show their appreciation in the support given to the organisation. The aspects that are customised by the organisation are those that are regarded as important by customers. Examples of this include the fabric and design of seats in a motor vehicle. This will provide added need satisfaction, and so will be supported by customers. There are, however, aspects in vehicles that customers would not appreciate. This would include the colour of the fabric used in the boot of the car.[21]

5.8.4 Adaptable Technology and Processes

The organisation has to have the machinery and equipment that can allow for customisation, e.g. that will allow the customer to order a specific fabric or seat design and incorporate it into the manufacture of the motor vehicle. This technology does not only refer to the ability to manufacture the product, but also to collect information about customers, interpret the information that has been collected and so offer meaningful customisation options that will provide need satisfaction to customers and increased profits to the organisation.

5.8.5 Support of Intermediaries and Suppliers

If an organisation is to implement a customisation programme, it will also require the support of the suppliers of raw materials and intermediaries in the distribution channel. Customisation requires changes in the ordering system, which requires greater adaptability and flexibility from suppliers. Intermediaries in the distribution channel have to be prepared to make the customisation options available to the customer, and this may require additional technology and training of retail staff.

> Assume that a motor vehicle manufacturer is giving customers options regarding interior seat design and fabric. This will mean the retail outlet must have the technology to record the preferences of its customers. The suppliers must be prepared to supply different amounts of fabric and parts for the manufacture of the seats as requested by customers. If existing suppliers are not prepared to supply differing volumes, the organisation may decide to use other suppliers who have greater flexibility.[22]

In addition to the above preconditions, two further preconditions can be identified as requirements for a mass customisation programme.[23]

- The first is the organisation's readiness for such a programme as reflected in the attitudes, culture and resources available for the mass customisation programme. Specific emphasis should be placed on the financial resources of the organisation.

- The second additional precondition is the competitive environment within which the organisation functions. This refers to the extent of the competition experienced by the organisation. The competitive environment may require that the organisation customise its products in order to sustain its competitive advantage.

5.9   Approaches to Mass Customisation

Once it has made the decision in principle to customise, there are a number of different approaches that an organisation can take. It has to decide the extent to which it wishes to customise the product, service or non-product aspects, as well as the communication sent to the consumer regarding the product. Each of the options have a different effect on the organisation, with some having a limited effect and others a major effect on the way in which the functions relate to each other. The decision has been made to customise, but the question is now: What should we customise?

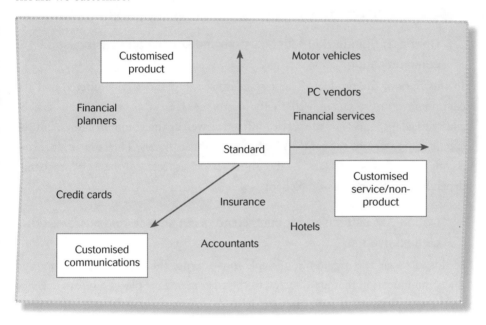

Figure 5.1 Approaches to Customisation[24]

Three distinct options exist for organisations:

Option 1: Standard product, standard service and customised communication

Option 2: Standard product, customised service and customised communication

Option 3: Customised product, customised service and customised communication.

Option 1: Standard product, standard service and customised communication

In this option, the organisation keeps the product and the nature of the service standardised, but adapts the communication, customising it to the customer it is attempting to reach. In this instance, the organisation is personalising the communication, and some organisations attempt to customise in this way. The impact of this personalisation is limited in that it does not affect the entire operation of the organisation.

Many e-retailers track the products purchased by their customers and adapt their communications to customers accordingly. Bookseller Amazon.com, for example, informs its customers electronically when titles by the same author are released. It is also able to suggest other authors that it believes the customer will enjoy, and communicates this directly to the customer using e-mails.

Option 2: Standard product, customised service and customised communication

In this option, the product is kept standardised, but the service offered and the communication are customised to the customer. Here the organisation has the ability to adapt aspects of the service offered as well as the communication, but the core product remains the same. An example of this is hotels. The core product that is offered remains constant, while the specific aspects of the service change depending on the needs of the client.

Option 3: Customised product, customised service and customised communication

In this instance, the organisation is able to customise the product, the service and the communication that are directed to the customer. This places a great challenge on the organisation, as it has to be able to deliver the options that it offers to its customer. This implies that the organisation's inter-functional co-ordination and co-operation have to be at a high level.

In the case of a motor vehicle, for example, the customer is able to choose the components of the product and the leasing arrangement that he/she wants, and the communication is aimed specifically at him/her.

5.10 Selecting the Appropriate Degree of Customisation

In customising the products, service components and communication, a decision regarding the extent to which each of these areas can be customised needs to be made. An organisation needs to examine various factors when deciding on the level of customisation that it will implement and the degree of customisation that it will offer. There are five main areas that need to be examined before implementing customisation.[25]

5.10.1 The Organisation's Mission (the Mandate Fit)

The issue that requires investigation is the mission and vision that the organisation has committed itself to in the marketplace. The mission reflects the reason for the existence of the business, and so it describes the way in which the organisation operates. In compiling its mission statement, the organisation is indicating the degree of customisation that is required.

> The mission statement for a financial services company might be as follows: 'To develop comprehensive financial services to our clients through their life cycle by developing relationships based on mutual trust and the harnessing of best-of-breed products, services and technology to ensure the highest level of client service.' This will reflect the degree of customisation that the organisation regards as appropriate for the industry in which it functions.

> Woolworths has the following vision: 'We aspire to being the most trusted and respected African retail brand. We will achieve this by nurturing and building lifetime relationships with our customers. These relationships will be earned by us all making the Woolies difference.'[26]

5.10.2 Customer Feasibility

The organisation has to carry out research into the needs of customers and the components of the product that they would like customised. Research will indicate the nature of the customisation customers want and the importance of this customisation to them. In order to do this, focus group research or behavioural segmentation can be used. This will enable people who exhibit similar behaviour to be conveniently grouped together. Each group's members would indicate their preferences with respect to the product, as well as the components of the product that they value. If customers do not value customisation of the product, customisation will not be worthwhile.

5.10.3 Competitive Advantage

One of the ways in which organisations can show a competitive advantage is through the implementation of customisation. Mass customisation can provide competitive advantage in three main areas:[27]

- Customers have wanted customisation for many years, but organisations have not been able to provide it or have been unwilling to provide it.

- Many organisations have yet to regard a 'segment of one' as being viable, and as a result, they have not developed a plan to deal with such a segment.

- Mass customisation is difficult to implement successfully, and as a result, organisations have not made a great deal of progress in implementing such a strategy.

In order to gain competitive advantage, it is necessary to examine the actions of the organisation's competitors and determine how the organisation wants to go about counteracting these actions in the marketplace. It is also necessary to determine the extent to which the competitors have customised, as well as the success with which this has been done.

5.10.4 Operational Feasibility

Once the organisation has determined that there is the need among its customers for customisation, and that this will provide a sustainable competitive advantage, it is necessary to ensure that it is possible for the organisation to actually carry out this customisation, i.e. whether the organisation has the ability to actually customise its products in the way that customers want. The machinery and equipment have to be able to cope with the pressures that customisation will place on them, as will the staff employed in this function. Any changes that have to be brought about will have a cost implication, which can affect the profitability of the organisation and hence the desirability of the customisation.

5.10.5 Financial Feasibility

This refers to the profitability that the customisation will bring to the organisation. Before customisation is implemented, it is essential that the organisation calculates the costs associated with it, as well as the potential benefits that can accrue to the organisation.

Benefits will be in the form of increased sales, as customers will be able to select the components that will best satisfy their needs. This will have an impact on their life-time value contribution to the organisation. This will also create the opportunity to bring out new variations of the customised product in the marketplace. It can also attract new customers to the organisation, increasing sales.

The costs associated with customisation are found in the changes in the technology that have to be made, the training of staff that has to take place and the changes in supply arrangements. The costs, both capital and operational, associated with customisation are very large. The organisation should implement customisation at the level that it can afford, and make the necessary adjustments.

5.11 Customisation and the Learning Relationship

The learning relationship (also see chapter 2) is a term used to describe a relationship between the customer and the organisation where the organisation gets 'smarter and smarter' with every contact made with a customer.[28] This means that customers are continually teaching the organisation what products they like and the nature of their consumption patterns.

This relationship works in that customers tell the organisation what they want through interaction and feedback. The organisation uses this information to adapt product specifications to satisfy the needs of customers, and then remembers the specifications.

For an organisation to create a learning relationship, there are two requirements that have to be met:[29]

- The organisation must be a successful customiser of its products. It must have the technology to be able to design further customisations, while also having the capacity to remember the preferences of its customers.

- Customers must be prepared to put in the effort to teach the organisation their specifications and preferences.

Unless the organisation continues learning about its customers (and vice versa), the relationship will not continue developing and growing, and the benefits that may accrue to the organisation will be reduced.

5.12 Summary

The purpose of the chapter was to examine the question of 1:1 marketing and mass customisation, and the relationship that exists between them.

After having defined 1:1 marketing, the difference between it and the traditional marketing approach was examined. The steps that make up the 1:1 marketing process were also discussed and identified.

Mass customisation was defined, and it was contrasted with personalisation as a strategy. In order to implement mass customisation, there are a number of preconditions that have to be met. Each of these preconditions was examined, as well as its effect on the customisation process. A number of customisation strategies were identified and the selection of the most appropriate strategy was examined.

Discussion Questions

1. Explain the term '1:1 marketing'.
2. Explain the difference between the terms 'market share' and 'share of customer'.
3. Explain the term 'economies of scope'.
4. Explain the difference between economies of scope and economies of scale. Why is this an important difference in the case of 1:1 marketing?
5. Explain the difference between mass marketing and 1:1 marketing.
6. Explain the steps in the 1:1 marketing process.
7. Explain the term 'mass customisation'.
8. Differentiate customisation and mass customisation from personalisation.
9. Explain the preconditions that are necessary for customisation to be implemented by an organisation.
10. Explain the three customisation strategies that an organisation can consider.
11. Explain the factors that affect the decision as to the extent of customisation that the organisation should consider.
12. Explain the relationship between customisation and competitive advantage.
13. Explain what is meant by a learning relationship. How does it impact on the customisation of the product?

Mini Case Study[30, 31]

Wesbank: Financing the used (pre-loved) car market

The motor vehicle industry in South Africa has a great deal of diversity. A number of manufacturers have local plants, and they are supplemented by those who provide motor vehicles that have been imported from foreign sources. Motor vehicle sales tend to be driven by the economy, because of the price of vehicles and the fact that they are acquired using credit facilities. It is these credit facilities that enable sales of motor vehicles to continue. Credit facilities are not only crucial in the sale of new cars, but the bulk of the financing granted on motor vehicles is on used motor vehicles. In the case of Wesbank, 65 per cent of vehicle financing is on used vehicles. This translates into a ratio of one new car for every 2.4 used vehicles financed.

The used vehicle market has changed in a number of ways. The negative perceptions associated with used cars is changing, as seen in the use of terms such as 'pre-owned' or 'pre-loved' to describe used cars. The way in which these vehicles are acquired is also changing. The use of technology makes it possible to search for vehicles online by using of the Internet, and credit approvals can also be done online.

Customers wanting to purchase used vehicles are evaluated using the same criteria. Financing a vehicle up to five years old has the same degree of risk as for a new vehicle, while the risk associated with financing older vehicles increases. As a result of this risk, the time period over which older vehicles are financed is reduced.

Questions

1. Is it feasible for Wesbank to make use of a 'segment of one' in its marketing? Motivate your answer adequately.

2. Is it a good idea for Wesbank to implement mass customisation? Motivate your answer adequately.

3. Explain three ways in which Wesbank could customise its service.

4. Explain how Wesbank can develop a learning relationship with its clients.

References

1   Pitta, DA. 1998. Marketing one to one and its dependence on knowledge discovery in databases. *Journal of Consumer Marketing*, 15 (5), pp. 468–80.
2   Peppers, D & Rogers, M. 1993. *The One-to-One Future*. London: Piatkus, p. 15.
3   Christopher, M, Payne, A & Ballantyne, D. 2002. *Relationship Marketing: Creating Stakeholder Value*. Oxford: Butterworth-Heinemann, p. 25.
4   Peppers & Rogers, *op. cit.*, p. 23.
5   Gummesson, E. 2002. *Total Relationship Marketing*. Oxford: Butterworth-Heinemann, p. 45.
6   Peppers & Rogers, *op. cit.*, p. 27.
7   *Ibid.*, p. 140.
8   *Ibid.*, p. 36.
9   Brink, A, Machado, R, Strydom, JW & Cant, MC. 2001. *Customer Relationship Management: Applied Strategy*. Study Guide 2. Pretoria: Unisa, p. 36.

10 Peppers & Rogers, *op. cit.*, p. 213.

11 *Ibid.*, p. 215.

12 Gordon, IH. 1998. *Relationship Marketing.* Toronto: John Wiley, p. 216.

13 *Ibid.*, p. 218.

14 Brink, *op. cit.*, p. 24.

15 Hart, CWL. 1995. Mass customisation: Conceptual underpinnings, opportunities and limits. *International Journal of Service Industry Management*, 6 (2), pp. 36–45.

16 Peppers, D & Rogers, M. 1997. *Enterprise One-to-One.* London: Piatkus, p. 148.

17 *Ibid.*, p. 142.

18 Gordon, *op. cit.*, p. 176.

19 *Ibid.*, p. 177.

20 Brink *et al.*, *op. cit.*, p. 25.

21 Gordon, *op. cit.*, p. 222.

22 *Ibid.*, p. 223.

23 Hart, *op. cit.*, p. 40.

24 Gordon, *op. cit.*, p. 224.

25 Brink *et al.*, *op. cit.*, pp. 31–34.

26 Woolworths. n.d. <http://www.woolworths.co.za>, accessed 10 January 2003.

27 Gordon, *op. cit.*, p. 236.

28 Peppers & Rogers, 1997, *op. cit.*, p. 15.

29 *Ibid.*, p. 170.

30 Furlonger, D. 2002. Motoring to the next milestone. *Financial Mail*, 1 November. <http://secure.financialmail.co.za/02/1101/cover/coverstoryd.html>, accessed 28 January 2003.

31 Furlonger, D. 2002. A new spring in the jalopy, as long as it's not too old. *Financial Mail*, 22 November. <http://secure.financialmail.co.za/02/1122/business.cbus.html>, accessed 28 January 2003.

CHAPTER

6

Business-to-Business
Marketing (B2B)

Learning Outcomes

After studying this chapter, you should be able to:

- contrast business and customer/consumer markets

- identify the conditions that are appropriate for the development of relationships between organisations

- explain the factors that impact on the efficiency of the organisation

- contrast the three types of relationship exchanges that exist within B2B

- comment on the relationships that organisations have with their business partners (suppliers, intermediaries and competitors)

- explain how relationships can be built with co-venture partners

- explain how e-commerce can be used as a tool in B2B.

6.1   Introduction

One of the most important relationships that an organisation can have takes place with other organisations. There are a number of different roles that other businesses can play within an organisation, and it is therefore necessary for the organisation to develop relationships with them.

6.2   B2B Markets and Their Composition

6.2.1   Consumer and Industrial Products

Consumer products are those products that are purchased by consumers for final consumption.[1] Examples of these products include toothpaste, chocolates and beer.

Industrial products are those products that are purchased by an organisation with the intention of using them to produce other goods and services. A number of different types of industrial products can be identified:

- **Mining products:** These are products that are taken from the earth, such as coal and iron ore, and that will be processed further.
- **Part-processed materials and components:** Further processing is generally necessary to use these products further, such as flour in baking products. Components are often assembled without any further changes being made to them, such as spark plugs and buttons.
- **Installations:** This includes capital equipment, buildings and heavy machinery, which are all expensive and which require large sums to be invested.
- **Accessory equipment:** This is equipment that is needed to make it possible to produce a final product, although it does not form part of the final product.
- **Operating supplies:** They are used either directly or indirectly in the production process, e.g. cleaning supplies, stationery and lubricants for machinery.

6.2.2   Differences between Consumer and Business Markets

Businesses deal with final consumers, yet one of their most important contacts is with other organisations. While it is necessary to develop relationships with both parties, the nature of the relationship is different as they involve different things. There are fundamental differences between doing business with consumers and doing business with other organisations. These differences are linked to the nature of these businesses and are reflected in table 6.1.[2]

Table 6.1 Final Consumers and Business Consumers: A Contrast

Final consumers	Business consumers
Goods are purchased for final consumption, and include speciality, shopping and convenience products.	Goods are purchased for production purposes and include components, accessory equipment and installations.
There are numerous consumers who individually are not able to exercise an influence on the organisation.	The market structure differs in that there are a few large consumers who exercise a large influence over the product.
Generally, use is made of intermediaries such as wholesalers and retailers.	The distribution channel for B2B activities is usually direct from the supplier to the organisation.
Consumers repurchase for a variety of reasons, which are as diverse as the people themselves.	There are a variety of purchasing situations such as straight rebuying, modified rebuying or new task buying.
Consumers make decisions regarding the suitability of the products to be purchased.	Purchasing decisions are usually made by a number of people who all have input into the final decision.
Customers are influenced by a wide variety of factors such as demographics and psychographic factors.	Organisations have a range of factors that they evaluate including, price and quality on offer.
These consumers are less likely to develop close relationships, as they are more fickle and more likely to switch brands.	Business consumers are more likely to develop close relationships, as organisations are recognised for their importance.
There is little likelihood of reciprocity of purchase.	Reciprocity is relatively common between organisations.
Mutual value creation is based on characteristics that are personal to the customer such as size and fit.	Mutual value creation is possible, as the businesses work together (as in the case of Intel and computer manufacturers).
Products such as low involvement products are one-way relationships.	There is higher interest in the relationships, though routine purchases may also be one-way relationships.

6.3   The Nature of CRM in B2B Markets

The question to ask is whether the supplier or any other business wants a relationship with the manufacturing organisation. For a relationship to develop, it is necessary to ensure that the relationship is wanted, and then go about developing this relationship. Examples of relationships include those with bankers, venture partners and competitors of the organisation.

6.3.1   Appropriate Conditions for Relationships between Organisations

Six essential conditions can be identified that influence the development of a relationship between organisations.[3] These conditions are interdependent and together impact on the desirability of the relationship.

- **Asymmetry:** This refers to the situation where one organisation can exert power over the other organisation. This would encourage the 'dominated' organisation to develop alternative links that will reduce the power being exercised by the more powerful organisation. This would enable the organisation to alter the balance of power.

> Assume Company X is the sole supplier of a specific raw material in South Africa. This will give it a great deal of power in the marketplace, as there is no other supplier that other companies can use.

- **Stability:** Relationships can be developed to decrease the instability experienced within the external environment. Organisations enter into long-term contracts in order to ensure a stable environment with respect to prices and delivery agreements.

> Many transport companies enter into long-term contracts with other businesses because of the size of the financial investment that transport requires. This means that a vehicle is purchased specifically for a specific contract and the transport company agrees to carry out the work at a specific price.

- **Legitimacy:** Being associated or having a relationship with a large, well-known organisation may improve the reputation of the smaller organisation. It can also reduce the checks that need to be carried out on such a small company, such as credit checks. This can increase the desirability of the relationship.

- **Necessity:** Organisations are required to use certain services such as those of auditors and accountants. Organisations tend to use the same accountants and auditors for extended periods of time, thereby developing a relationship with them.

- **Reciprocity:** This refers to the relationship that develops where one organisation buy the goods of the other, and vice versa.[4] This enables both organisations to pursue common goals, so that both organisations benefit. This in turn contributes to the development of a relationship.

- **Efficiency:** This is an internal contingency and refers to the way in which business is carried out in an organisation. There are three aspects that affect the efficiency within an organisation.

1. Types of costs associated with transactions

A variety of costs can be identified when carrying out transactions. Co-ordination costs are those costs incurred in investigating other organisations to determine whether to do business with them, such as investigating their creditworthiness. Motivation costs refer to the lack of completeness that an organisation may experience when carrying out an investigation. Another type of motivation cost occurs when one party shows that it is not fully committed to the relationship — which implies that its promises may not be kept.

2. The level of transaction costs

The level of transaction costs is affected by a number of factors, including opportunistic behaviour, moral hazard and bounded rationality. Opportunistic behaviour refers to the situation where one organisation exploits the situation to its own advantage, as there are terms and conditions within the contract that have not been met. Moral hazard exists when the other party in the agreement monitors the agreement, and so ensures that it is not exploited. (Should the other party attempt to do so, it will hesitate to do so, as it is aware of being monitored within the terms of the agreement.) Bounded rationality comes about with the inability to factor in all possible outcomes within a situation, and so these situations have not been described totally within the contract.

3. The dimensions of transactions

Transactions have seven dimensions that affect their nature, which in turn affects the nature of the relationship between the organisations.

- Asset specificity: This is when a transaction requires a specific item in order to enter into the agreement. This will also affect the management of the contract over time, as the investment in assets will require that a certain price level be maintained.

> In the case of a high degree of asset specificity, where an organisation has spent a great deal of money on acquiring the required assets, it will only do so if it is sure that it will win the contract from the other organisation.

- **Frequency of transactions:** If it is a regular supply arrangement, a traditional contract of agreement will be drawn up. Should the contract be a once-off contract of high value, the organisation may spend money on drawing up a specific contract in order to specify the actions of both parties.

- **Duration of transactions:** If transactions take place over long periods of time, the relationship that develops is a much deeper one, and so an understanding develops between the parties.

- **Complexity of the transaction:** When a product has been customised, costs can be added to the transaction by making minor changes or adjustments.

- **Monitoring of a contract:** Because it is not possible to predict every action of a party in a relationship, the contract has to be monitored in order to ensure that both parties fulfil the terms and conditions associated with their activities.

- **The measurement of actual performance:** This is required to determine whether the parties are performing as they are required to perform. The measurement of the actual performance has to be accurate, while also indicating the existence of any possible problems, should they exist. Measuring the actual performance must be done in a cost-effective way in order to maximise efficiency.

- **The interrelatedness (connectedness) of transactions:** Decisions on the purchase of one item can affect the purchase of another item, and this makes the purchase decision a connected decision. Not all decisions are connected, and the degree of connectedness makes it necessary to examine the decision-making variables connected with each decision.

6.3.2 Types of relationships in B2B

When building relationship with other business organisations, a decision has to be made concerning the nature of the relationship that will be developed. Three main business relationships exist, as indicated in figure 6.1. The continuum reflects extremes in the relationship that develops, with an anonymous relationship on one end of the continuum and a collaborative relationship on the other end.

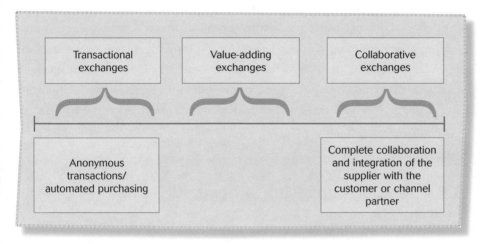

Figure 6.1 The Relationship Spectrum[5]

Transactional exchanges refer to the anonymous purchasing that takes place between people, as in the case of the purchase of stationery and cleaning materials. In the example of stationery, each person obtains what he/she wants (the seller obtains money and the buyer obtains stationery). The transactional exchange centres on the timely exchange of basic goods at competitive prices.[6] These exchanges are formal, and competitive bidding can be used to determine the best prices.

At the opposite end of the continuum are the *collaborative exchanges* that develop between organisations. This collaboration is such that both parties work together to form very close links and relationships so that both parties are able to derive the maximum long-term benefits from the relationship. This will include joint problem solving and information sharing, and there will be a high degree of commitment from both parties.

In the example of a large cement organisation that transports its goods for export by rail, it has an arrangement with the rail company that rail trucks will be supplied at a particular time and at a particular price. Should both parties complete their tasks as originally specified, the cement company receives quality service while the rail company has an income from its client. If the cement company does not fill the trucks within a specified period, it is charged a higher price because of the new arrangements that are required from the rail company. If the trucks are not delivered by a certain time, the cement company can obtain a discount on the transport costs.

Value-added exchanges lie between transactional and collaborative exchanges. Here the aim of the organisation changes from that of finding clients to retaining clients, and so building a relationship with them.[7] This requires that the business investigates its client's needs and adapts its product to suit these needs.

As organisations move on the relationship spectrum, the nature of the relationship will change. In the case of collaborative exchanges, the development and maintenance of trust is vital, as is the commitment of the parties to the relationship. (Relationship commitment can be defined as *the belief by a partner that an ongoing relationship is important, and so it requires maximum efforts to maintain the relationship.*)[8]

6.4   Relationships with Specific B2B Markets

6.4.1 Suppliers

One of the key relationships that organisations build is with their suppliers. The supply chain illustrates the wider network of role-players — from those who supply the raw materials, to those who carry out the entire transformation process, through to the consumer.[9] Here, organisations do not compete with each other on an individual basis; rather, they compete according to the efficiency within the supply chain. This means that if an organisation wants to increase its competitiveness in the marketplace, it can be done through developing close relationship with the suppliers of the raw materials and services, in order to make the supply chain more efficient for them.

The importance of suppliers to the organisation can be seen in a number of areas:[10]

- the quality of the product supplied, which affects the quality of the final product;
- the quantity of the product supplied, which affects the availability of the product in the marketplace;
- the price, which affects the final selling price in the marketplace; and
- the timing, which affects the product schedule according to which manufacturing can take place.

There has been a change in the marketplace as to how organisations treat their suppliers. In the past, organisations tended to keep their suppliers 'on their toes' and did not commit themselves too much, in order to avoid giving suppliers any power over them. This has changed to reflect a higher degree of collaboration and co-operation between the suppliers and organisations. Co-makership is a strategy that organisations are implementing in order to improve relationships with suppliers. Co-makership *is the decision to limit the number of suppliers with whom the organisation will do business.*[11] This results in closer relationships developing with the suppliers, as there is a greater degree of commitment and involvement between suppliers and organisations. This reduces the friction in the relationship and replaces it with a co-operative spirit that results in greater profitability for all parties.

The reason for this change is the understanding that greater benefits can accrue for both parties as a result of this approach. The organisation is able to provide more information about its customers, and this enables the suppliers to provide products that are more suitable to the customers. This benefits both the suppliers and the organisation from a customer satisfaction perspective as well as from a financial perspective. This also enables the organisation to develop products with the supplier for introduction into the market.[12]

The importance of developing sound relationships with suppliers is seen in the amounts of attention and money that are invested in developing information and other systems that can improve the delivery of products to the organisation from the supplier.

> In 1998, Wooltru and Datatec entered into a joint venture, Affinity Logic. This enables Massmart (Makro and Dion) and Wooltru to make use of the technology offered by Affinity Logic. Affinity managed their IT, finance, administration, payrolls and logistics functions. The contract has been concluded for ten years and is estimated to be worth R10 billion.[13]

In the case of CRM, one of the important suppliers is the supplier of the database management system that is used by the organisation. Through data mining and effective data management, an organisation can examine its customer database and so make sense of the information that it has collected.

> In the case of banks and retail stores, they both have accounts and charge cards that provide these organisations with information about their customers. The extensive information that they have must be interpreted if it to be used to the advantage of the organisations. This information will not only clarify the

nature of each customer and his/her activities, but it can be used to refine the supply chain. This may result in removing the suppliers of certain goods and replacing them with other suppliers, or suppliers of products that will better satisfy customer needs.

Specific guidelines can be proposed regarding how to develop a relationship with suppliers. Many of the guidelines are common to relationships in general, such as communication, trust and commitment. Also, databases can be developed to the advantage of both parties, while sharing market and customer information can also improve the relationship.

6.4.2 Intermediaries

Intermediaries are *those organisations in the distribution channel who help the product get to the marketplace.* They include retailers, wholesalers and agents who have contact with customers.[14] The key to the success of an organisation can be found in the supply chain, of which the intermediaries are an important part. To improve its relationship with intermediaries, the organisation needs to treat them as it would treat its best customers, and not just to treat them as part of the process. This means that all strategies that are used in dealings with final consumers are used in building relationships with intermediaries.[15]

The complication in the process comes from the fact that the goals of the intermediary and the organisation may be different, making the relationship more challenging.

Keys to managing the relationship with intermediaries are as follows:[16]

- Planning undertaken by both the organisation and the intermediary can help to improve the relationship. This can support the intermediary, who tends to have a less-developed planning process (than the organisation).
- Channel-member profitability also needs the attention of the organisation. It can develop ways of improving profits, while the intermediary can alert the organisation to additional marketing opportunities.
- Respect and trust are further components of this process. As in any relationship, without trust between the two parties, the relationship will not develop and improve. This includes clear and open communication between the parties.
- The intermediary is the customer – but is often treated as if he/she were more of a nuisance than a customer. This would indicate that the organisation does

not have power over the intermediary. But despite the fact that both the organisation and the intermediary are independent organisations, there is a high degree of interdependence between them.

 Keep the focus on the final customer. Despite each of them (the organisation and the intermediary) having specific goals that they wish to achieve, the focus needs to remain on the final consumers and the satisfaction of their needs.

6.4.3 Competitors

The concept of building relationships with competitors sounds strange to many people. Competitors are *other organisations who sell similar goods and services to similar consumers*.[17] Competitors are either direct competitors, or they are involved in selling a substitute product that will also satisfy customers' needs. The idea that you build a relationship with another organisation that is seeking to attract your existing customers initially does not sound like good business sense. However, when organisations take on their competitors in the marketplace, a situation often arises that is not to the long-term benefit of anyone. This situation could include price wars, loss of reputation and the wasting of organisational resources. This conflict has the potential of undermining the entire industry, as the confidence of customers is also shaken, and the profits in the industry can also suffer.[18] If an industry is unregulated, cut-throat price competition may take place, resulting in bankruptcies among smaller organisations.[19]

> The airline industry in South Africa in the domestic market has been experiencing difficulties for some time with respect to profits and sustainability. New airlines have come and gone. Examples of these include (the original) Sun Air and Phoenix. The original Sun Air closed weeks after South African Airways had purchased a 75 per cent stake in the airline, bringing SAA's motives into question.[20]

Before making a decision regarding the relationships with competitors, the organisation must ensure that it is fully informed about the products and target markets of their competitors.[21] This will ensure that it can anticipate its competitors' actions and plan its own response in advance. Linked to this is the importance of ensuring that marketing information is continually gathered about competitors and their planned actions.

Collecting information concerning competitors will ensure that the organisation can determine a 'competitor profile' for each of its competitors. This will aid in determining how its competitors will react to its own strategies. From this competitor profile, the organisation will know who the competitors are who will:

- fight to the death;
- engage in a counterattack (and the form this will take); or
- ignore the actions of any competitor.

From the information gathered about competitors, it will be clear what the various competitors' strengths and weaknesses are, and how they can be exploited.[22]

> Examples in the airline industry of strategic alliances are numerous. Examples include British Airways and Comair, SAA and Lufthansa, and SAA and Qantas. These alliances have been forged in the interests of both profitability and sustainability, while satisfying customer needs.

6.4.4 Co-venture Partners and Strategic Alliances

An alliance is defined as *an arrangement for organised and agreed relations between parties,* such as exists between customers, partners and competitors.[23] These alliances mean that co-operation takes place between the parties in the alliance.

Co-venture partners provide an organisation with the opportunity of exploiting a situation without having to carry all the risk and expense itself. It enables the organisation to exploit synergies that exist between the two parties. These relationships are not necessarily traditional relationships, as the partners may be involved in selling related products and services. By developing the partnership, access can be obtained to another group of customers. Organisations can also have help in obtaining economies of scale, as well as in sharing risk.[24]

> An example of creating partnerships is seen in the alliances Xerox has forged with other companies. In the UK, Europe and Africa, Xerox has allied itself with Rank, while in India and Japan, it has allied itself with Fuji and Modi.[25]

The question can be posed: What makes a successful strategic alliance? Two critical success factors can contribute to a successful relationship:[26]

- **A close working relationship:** Without a close working relationship between the parties, long-term success is not possible. This means that the parties are required to communicate frequently and deal with important issues that affect both parties.

- **Integrating points of contact:** The approach that the organisations use must be flexible in that it must be able to incorporate changes in the environment and in circumstances that have been identified. The integration between the two organisations needs to be strategic, tactical, operational, interpersonal and cultural. By developing these interactions, the organisations will be able to ensure that the relationship continues to develop and to achieve the goals that have been set by both organisations.

6.5 Managing Relationships Effectively

There is little point in establishing relationships with other businesses and then not managing them effectively. As with all relationships, it is necessary to put in effort on a continual basis to ensure that the relationship stays positive. This indicates that relationship management is a continual process with which managers are engaged.

There are four requirements that indicate whether a relationship is being effectively managed:[27]

- **Awareness:** Within the relationship, it is important that the manager has an awareness of the problems and opportunities that form part of the relationship, as well as of the expectations of the other party in the relationship.

- **Assessment:** This refers to the continual evaluation of the resources that the organisation has to offer in terms of resources that are needed to get to the destination both parties are aiming for.

- **Accountability:** To ensure that relationships are maintained, it is necessary to establish reporting procedures regarding the state of the relationship, as well as the performance of the relationship.

- **Actions:** All actions must be evaluated in terms of their potential impact on the organisational relationship. This means that the consequences of any action need to be determined so as to ensure they do not harm the relationship in any way.

6.6 e-Commerce as a Tool in Managing Business Relationships

Probably one of the most widely used tools for managing business relationships is the use of e-commerce and electronic sites to facilitate interaction between the partners. It is estimated that 90 per cent of all e-commerce carried out online in 1999 involved B2B deals, and they were worth approximately $433 billion.[28] It is further estimated that 26 per cent of all organisations bought goods online.[29] e-Commerce is not about the sales that can be generated, but must be used to make a connection with business partners. It is also not about a transaction, but is rather a process with which the organisation is involved. The e-commerce forum enables organisations to reach new markets at lower costs.[30]

There are a number of factors that need to be evaluated when examining a particular exchange (B2B site). These factors include:[31]

- **The target market:** Those organisations that target large organisations do not have the support services to service small businesses. Having a large corporation as the target market implies that it has the IT to make a connection possible.

- **Focus:** Vertically focused exchanges tend to focus on the provision of credit risk management and bill payment. Horizontally focused exchanges take place with service providers offering mediated services that companies need.

- **Purpose:** This refers to the problem that the exchange seeks to solve. This should thus provide some value-added service to add to existing functions.

- **Profitability:** It is important to understand how the exchange will generate revenue (and hence profitability for the organisation).

- **Community size opportunity:** Only serving a very small community may endanger the existence of the exchange. This means that the exchange has to show opportunity for growth if it is to remain viable.

- **Implementation:** The organisation must commit adequate resources to the exchange to ensure that it is able to fulfil its purpose.

- **Management team:** The management team has to be able to lead the exchange towards improving the relationship with other businesses, and so be able to deliver what is necessary for the success of the exchange.

6.7 Summary

B2B is one of the most important relationships that an organisation can build with another party. It is important to take note of the differences that exist between final customers and business customers and the impact that this has on relationship building. Not all businesses want to develop relationships, and the situation must be conducive to the building of such relationships. Relationships can be built with a number of other businesses, including intermediaries, suppliers and co-venture partners. Tools used in this building process include e-commerce.

Discussion Questions

1. Explain the term 'B2B'.
2. Explain the term 'industrial products' and their components.
3. Explain the difference between final consumers and business consumers. Indicate three main differences.
4. Name six conditions that can be used to determine the desirability of relationships between organisations.
5. 'Organisational efficiency is a very important component of relationship building.' Explain this statement, indicating whether you agree with it or not.
6. Explain the term 'relationship spectrum', using a diagram to illustrate your answer.
7. Why do you think an organisation should build relationships with its intermediaries?
8. 'The relationship with competitors is a very important one to build.' Explain this statement, indicating whether or not you agree with it.
9. Discuss the nature of a strategic alliance. Illustrate the importance of this relationship.
10. What critical success factors can determine whether an alliance is successful?
11. What strategies can managers use to effectively manage a B2B relationship?
12. What is meant by e-commerce? How can it be used to develop relationships with other organisations?

Mini Case Study

Unitrans Ltd

Unitrans Ltd is a diversified transport, distribution and logistics group that is active in freight and passenger transport, warehousing, distribution and logistics services.[32] Its vision is 'to be rated by our stakeholders as the most innovative provider of transportation, distribution and logistical solutions in our chosen markets'.[33]

United Transport purchased Thornton's Transport to form Unitrans in 1962. In the 1980s, Sanlam became the sole shareholder, while the passenger transport division was sold to Tollgate Holdings in 1987.[34] Today, there are a number of divisions within the Unitrans Group. They can be illustrated as follows:

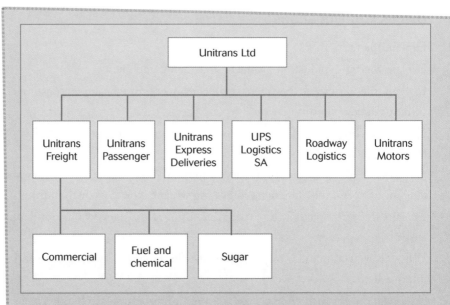

Figure 6.2 The Organisational Structure of Unitrans[35]

The Unitrans Freight arm has a number of different clients that produce a diverse range of products such as paper, metals and minerals, as well as drinks. One of the main areas of Unitrans's activity is the transportation of fuels such as diesel and petrol from the coast to inland areas, as well as into neighbouring states. In the past, all fuel was carried by what is today Spoornet, but Unitrans is able to offer fuel companies flexibility in the service offered. Unitrans transports fuels from the Caltex depots in Cape Town, Total's products from its Alrode depot, and from BP's operations in East London and Port Elizabeth. In the case of the transportation of chemicals such as caustic soda, special equipment and driver training are required to reduce the hazards associated with their transportation. Key clients include Sasol Solvents and Polifin. From its Durban base, Unitrans operates 110 vehicles and 200 trailers, delivering products throughout South Africa and its neighbouring countries. The importance of logistics partnerships has been identified by Sasol. Its logistics manager, Mr Khobo, states: 'It is more than just transporting and storing products. It involves building close relationships and working with service suppliers.'[36]

Questions

1. Assuming you are the manager of Total (or Caltex), discuss the nature of the relationship that you would want with Unitrans.

2. As the divisional manager of Unitrans Freight, how would you go about building relationships with the company's various key clients?

3. As a CRM consultant, you want to advise Unitrans to develop a relationship with its competitors, namely the Imperial Group and Supergroup. Motivate this suggestion to Mr Jo Grové, the Unitrans CEO.

References

1   Van der Walt, A, Strydom, JW, Marx, S & Jooste, CJ. 1996. *Marketing Management* (3rd ed.). Cape Town: Juta.

2   Gordon, IH. 1998. *Relationship Marketing.* Toronto: John Wiley, pp. 114–33.

3   Blois, KJ. 1996. Relationship marketing in organisational markets: When is it appropriate? *Journal of Marketing Management*, 12, pp. 161–73.

4   Gordon, *op. cit.*, p. 128.

5   Day, GS. 2000. Managing market relationships. *Journal of the Academy of Marketing Science*, 28 (1), p. 25.

6   Hutt, MD & Speh, TW. 2001. *Business Marketing Management.* Fort Worth: Harcourt College Publishers, p. 89.

7   Day, *op. cit.*, p. 25.

8   Hutt & Speh, *op. cit.*, p. 90.

9   Nieman, G & Bennett, A (eds). 2002. *Business Management: A Value Chain Approach.* Pretoria: Van Schaik, p. 17.

10   Cronje, GJ de J, Du Toit, GS & Motlana, MDC. 2000. *Introduction to Business Management* (5th ed.). Cape Town: Oxford University Press, p. 422.

11   Du Plessis *et al.*, *op. cit.*, p. 282.

12   Christopher, M, Payne, A & Ballantyne, D. 2002. *Relationship Marketing: Creating Stakeholder Value.* Oxford: Butterworth-Heinemann.

13   Bidoli, M. 1998. Laying the IT foundation for retail innovation. *Financial Mail.* <http://www.secure.financialmail.co.za/98/1016/invest/wool.html>, accessed 20 July 2003.

14   Peck, H, Payne, A, Christopher, M & Clark, M. 2004. *Relationship Marketing Strategy and Implementation.* Amsterdam: Elsevier Butterworth-Heinemann, p. 34.

15   *Ibid.*

16   Du Plessis, PJ, Jooste, CJ & Strydom, JW. 2001. *Applied Strategic Marketing.* Sandown: Heinemann.

17   Cronje *et al.*, *op. cit.*, p. 69.

18   Du Plessis, *et al.*, *op. cit.*

19   Gummesson, E. 2002. *Total Relationship Marketing.* Oxford: Butterworth-Heinemann.

20   Eedes, J. 2002. An exclusive phoenix rises. *Financial Mail*, 18 January. <http://secure.financialmail.co.za/02/0118/focus.efocus.html>, accessed 11 June 2003.

21   Du Plessis *et al.*, *op. cit.*, p. 289.

22   *Ibid.*, p. 290.

23 Gummesson, *op. cit.*, p. 157.

24 Hutt & Speh, *op. cit.*, p. 102.

25 Gummesson, *op. cit.*, p. 158.

26 Hutt & Speh, *op. cit.*, p. 105.

27 Payne, A, Christopher, M, Clark, M & Peck, H. 2001. *Relationship Marketing for Competitive Advantage.* Oxford: Butterworth-Heinemann.

28 Enos, L. 2003. The biggest myths about B2B. *e-Commerce News.* <http://www.ecommercetimes.com/perl/story/11327.html>, accessed 10 June 2003.

29 Kioa, K. ISM/Forrestoer Research announce results of latest report on eBusiness. <http://ism.ws/ISMReport/Forrester/FROB012002PR.cfm>, accessed 10 June 2003.

30 Kenjale, K & Phatek, A. 2002. The benefit of B2B exchanges. <http://www.destinationcrm.com/articles/default.asp?ArticleID=2698>, accessed 10 June 2003.

31 Morgenthal, JP. 2001. Which B2B exchange is right for you? <http://softwaremag.com/archive/2001feb/SelectinB2BExchange.html>, accessed 10 June 2003.

32 Unitrans. n.d. <http://www.unitrans.co.za/organisation/main_org.html>, accessed 24 June 2003.

33 Unitrans. n.d. <http://www.unitrans.co.za/organisation/org_vision.html>, accessed 24 June 2003.

34 *Financial Mail*, special survey, 17 March 2000. <http://fm.co.za>, accessed 24 June 2003.

35 Unitans, <http://www.unitrans.co.za/organisation/main_org.html>, *op. cit.*

36 Financial Mail, *op. cit.*

CHAPTER

7

Stakeholders in Relationship Marketing

Learning Outcomes

After studying this chapter, you should be able to:

- explain the nature of stakeholders and their importance in relationship building

- explain the term 'stakeholders' and differentiate it from shareholders in an organisation

- identify the composition of a lateral partnership

- discuss the importance of these lateral partnerships to an organisation

- comment on the developments in South Africa regarding lateral partnerships

- explain the importance of the following specific lateral partnerships to an organisation:

    ◆ investors

    ◆ environmental stakeholders

    ◆ the community

    ◆ the media

- show how organisations can build relationships with lateral partners.

7.1   Introduction

The definition of relationship marketing given in chapter 1 identified the building of relationships with customers as well as with other *stakeholders*, and it is these stakeholders that are the focus of this chapter. We will see that building relationships with these stakeholders is critically important to an organisation and that the quality of these relationships affects the organisation and its profitability. This chapter will investigate the specific relationships the organisation should build, while also suggesting ways they can be developed.

7.2   Stakeholders and CRM: A Definition

When examining the groups with whom the organisation aims to build relationships, the term 'stakeholder' is used to describe *any party or group who is able to influence (affect) or be influenced (affected) by the organisation and its activites.*[1] This definition indicates that the use of the word 'stakeholders' means more than just the shareholders (people who have invested money in the business), and thus is a much wider term. Stakeholders are thus interested in how projects are carried out (through the efforts of their employees), as well as the outcome of these projects (shareholders, community and government).[2]

Using the term 'stakeholder' has major implications for an organisation, as it means there are many groups with whom the organisation seeks to build relationships. This means that the organisation has to determine priorities in its relationship building and build relationships in an integrated way.[3] This can be difficult, as these stakeholders affect different parts of the organisation, and so interact with different managerial groupings. For example, trade unions may interact with the human resources department (and managers) in the organisation, while suppliers interact with representatives of the purchasing department. Without a unified approach to building relationships with stakeholders, the organisation does not receive the benefit of these relationships. It will be clear from the discussion in this chapter that relationship building takes place within the context of the organisation's activities, missions and values. Building relationships with these groups is also not just the task of the marketing department, but includes the actions of top management.

These stakeholders have also been described as being 'strategically significant' to the organisation. This comment is made due to the influence that these stakeholders can have on the functioning of the organisation, as well as on its survival.

7.3 The Composition of Stakeholders

There have been many attempts to represent the relationship between stakeholders who influence the organisation and the organisation itself. Examples of these attempts include the Six Markets model[4] and the Relational Exchanges model proposed by Morgan and Hunt.[5] The stakeholders identified in relationship marketing are shown in figure 7.1. In this diagram, these stakeholders are identified as a 'lateral partnership', and they will be the focus of this chapter. (The other partnerships shown in figure 7.1 have been discussed in previous chapters, as indicated in the figure.)

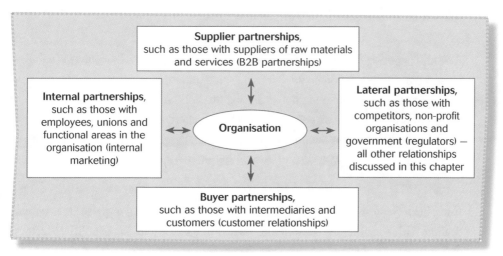

Figure 7.1 The Stakeholders in Relationship Marketing[6, 7]

There are a number of important aspects to note in figure 7.1.

- Firstly, the organisation is central in the relationship-building process between the organisation and its stakeholders, and is therefore placed in the centre of the figure.

- Secondly, there is a mutually dependent relationship between the organisation and the stakeholders identified as lateral partnerships. This is seen in the mutual influence that the parties have on one another. This means that the organisation not only influences a specific stakeholder, but that the stakeholder has an impact on the activities of the organisation.

- Thirdly, the groups of stakeholders influence one another, meaning that there is no stakeholder group that doesn't have an influence on (or isn't influenced by) another stakeholder group. This is seen, for example, in the effect that the government has on the supplier and buyer partnerships. Supplier partnerships affect the lateral partnerships, while also affecting internal and buyer partnerships. Examples that are supplied in this chapter show how public and environmental concerns cannot be separated, but, in fact, have a mutual influence on each other.

7.4 The Nature and Importance of Lateral Partnerships to the Organisation

Stakeholders are important to an organisation, as their actions can affect the organisation. Without their support regarding certain key actions, the organisation will not be able to successfully implement a course of action.

> If one uses a car-manufacturing company as an example, if it wants to build a new plant in an environmentally sensitive area, the media have the power to influence the opinion of the public against this course of action. Further, protests by environmentalists will negatively affect public perceptions of the organisation. The shareholders may support the programme from a financial perspective, but veto it because of the actions of these other groups

It has been suggested that South African organisations do well in these areas (when dealing with social and governmental issues) due to various socio-political factors in South Africa.

7.5 Significant Developments Relating to Lateral Partnerships

7.5.1 The Triple Bottom Line

The term 'bottom line' is well known when referring to the profits of an organisation, but the term 'triple bottom line' (TBL) is now becoming commonplace. TBL refers to the scorecard where organisations have to report on an organisation's environmental, social and economic performance.[8] TBL is regarded as a component of good governance, while also being a result of good governance in a previous period.[9]

Economic reporting is more than reporting on financial performance, but needs to include supply chain, staff training and development, as well as economic value added.[10] Social reporting is not just about the social-responsibility spending of the organisation, but includes the interests of stakeholders such as communities and government and the 'licence to operate' in the society.[11]

The problem with having to report on the TBL is that many social and environmental effects cannot be measured, but despite this, these initiatives and the reporting on them are critical to the stakeholders.[12] The reporting on these matters can be time-consuming, and the challenge for the organisation is to streamline their reporting structures.[13] Some executives use this as a reason to delist from the stock exchange (which insists on TBL reporting), justifying this by saying that what the organisation does is 'nobody's business but its own'.[14] Criticism has also been levelled that TBL is a reason for the development of associated industries such as public relations practitioners who 'feed off industry'.[15]

7.5.2 The King II Report

The King I report (named after its chairman, Mervyn King), was first published in 1994, followed by the *King Report on Corporate Governance* in 2004 (known as King II).[16] The purpose of this report is to focus on corporate governance in organisations, focusing on how they should be managed. King II is focused on all public companies, banks and financial organisations, as well as certain public sector enterprises. It comments on the use of integrated sustainability reporting (another term for TBL reporting) to achieve a balance among the organisation's economic, social and environmental performances. The King report specifies the contents of this integrated sustainability reporting, while also providing for enforcement of the code of conduct governing this kind of reporting.

7.5.3 Broad-based Black Economic Empowerment (BBBEE)

BBBEE and BEE (black economic empowerment) are strategies of government linked to the political transformation objectives in society. (This topic results in an emotive discussion among citizens, and the purpose of its inclusion here is to focus on its effect on relationship building.) The purpose behind these government strategies is to promote the achievement of the constitutional right of all South Africans to equality by increasing the participation of black people in the economy, which results in a more equitable distribution of income.[17, 18] Based on this policy, scorecards and charters have been developed to guide the implementation of BBBEE. The effect of these codes is that an organisation has to examine its ownership (shareholders), management and suppliers who contribute to the organisation's success. The effect of this bill is that the organisation has to build relationships with different parties than those of the past, and may require new approaches to relationship building.

7.6 Specific Lateral Partners Who Affect the Organisation

Stakeholders have specific expectations of an organisation, as reflected in table 7.1.

Table 7.1 Expectations of Specific Stakeholders[19]

Stakeholder group	Primary expectation	Secondary expectation
Shareholders	Financial returns	Added value
Community	Safety and security	Contribution to the community
Government	Compliance	Improved competitiveness

Should these expectations not be met, the stakeholders will act in a way that indicates to the organisation that their expectations are not being met. In this way, a shareholder may sell shares, the community may protest, while the government may develop legislation or regulations to change this situation.

7.6.1 Investors and Financial Stakeholders (Shareholders)

In many cases, marketers do not pay much attention to shareholders, believing this to be the task of management or public relations practitioners. However, the development of relationship marketing has brought this group to the attention of marketers as a relationship group. There are some that believe this group is only important for companies that are listed on the stock exchange, such as public companies.[20] It must be remembered that every organisation has investors, even if they are SMEs (small or medium-sized enterprises), and it remains their task to build relationships with this group. Further, with the transformation objectives associated with BBBEE, there are people owning shares who have never been involved in this way previously.

The role of the shareholder is to provide funds to the organisation, which are used in the development of the organisation's activities. The reason for investing in the organisation is the generation of returns on the investment made. A number of financial methods have been developed and are used to measure the value that the organisation creates for its shareholders, such as economic value added (EVA) and shareholder value added (SVA).[21]

Despite the importance of shareholders, it has been suggested that organisations have problems when building relationships with investors. The main reason for this is investor churn, i.e. the constant change of investors, as people buy and sell shares in the company. It has been suggested that the average public company in the USA has an investor churn of 50 per cent (or more) per year.[22] The reason why shareholders invest in the first place, i.e. to generate profits in the short term, is often the cause of this. Should these returns not be generated, investors sell their shares, and shareholder churn is the result.

For a South African organisation, a number of target markets for investor relations can be identified:

- **Johannesburg Securities Exchange:** Whether an organisation is listed on the main board or on the alternative board (AltX), the JSE is an important stakeholder group.

- **Investors (present and future):** These are the people who have invested their money in the organisation with the intention of generating returns (in the form of share price increases and dividends).[23]

- **Employees:** These would be employees who have been given shares, sometimes as part of the organisation's BBBEE (or BEE) programme.

- **Customers**: The people currently buying an organisation's product may like the product so much that they decide to invest in the organisation, and so want information regarding its financial performance.

- **Suppliers:** Suppliers want to make sure that they will be paid, and so knowledge of the organisation's financial situation is important to them.

In managing this relationship, it has been suggested that organisations make use of an investor relations manager, but this may not be adequate for the scope and importance of the task.[24] Not everyone is convinced that investor relationships are very important. It has been suggested that the only thing that is important to an investor are the financial statements reflecting profit and cash-flow situations.[25] It has been suggested that everything besides the financial data is 'just spin'.[26]

Shareholder activism is increasing in South Africa, and law suits have resulted on some occasions, where the shareholders have taken directors of organisation to court and often won their cases.[27] On one occasion, Old Mutual put in an offer for the minority shares in Mutual & Federal at a discount to the ruling price. This caused the shareholders to protest, and the board of Mutual & Federal rejected the offer.[28]

In building relationships with investors, it has been suggested that the organisation should make use of the RACE formula.[29] This formula consists of a number of key steps:

- **Research:** When wanting to build relationships with the investor, it is necessary to carry out research as to what types of investors have put money into the organisation, what their needs and perspectives are, and what types of information they would like to have.

- **Analysis:** Once the organisation knows what types of investors have put money into it, it is necessary to examine closely their needs and their responses. These will be incorporated into the organisation's communications with investors.

- **Communication:** This refers to the messages that are sent to the investors, as well as the integration of the messages with the activities of the organisation. The organisation has to communicate with its shareholders using media that reach them. This would include the Internet (through the investor relations tab), as well as the financial media.

- **Evaluation:** Here the communication is evaluated to determine whether a specific medium actually reaches the target audience, while also determining the quality of the communication with the market. The relationship quality and the behaviours of the investors that result from the communication can also be evaluated. Even if the investor sells his/her shares, the quality of the relationship that existed at the time he/she did so can also be evaluated, as the needs of the shareholder will determine when the shares were sold, and this is important information for the organisation to know.

7.6.2 Environmental Stakeholders

With any manufacturing organisation, there is always the question of environmental issues. Environmentalism and the focus on global warming have placed the environment on the agenda for all organisations.

Environmental stakeholders are not equally important to all organisations, as their importance depends primarily on the nature of the organisation's activities. This makes the environmental stakeholders critical to manufacturing organisations, and petrochemical and mining companies.[30]

The power of environmental stakeholders differs throughout the world. In the more developed economies, the power of these stakeholders is higher than in developing economies. Generally, however, these stakeholders are beginning to exercise more power and influence over businesses' activities. Members of the public are also aware of the importance of the environment and so are also being influenced by these groups. This has resulted in a greater degree of activism, which can cause damage to the organisation's assets.[31]

> The effect of poor environmental management can be felt on the bottom line of the organisation. Iscor (now Mittal Steel) was sued by the residents of Vanderbijlpark for causing pollution in the area and the company settled out of court for R33 million. Cape PLC had to pay out £22 million (about R240 million) to workers as compensation for the asbestosis that workers contracted from working on its mines.[32]

7.6.3 The Community

Organisations are established in areas where, by implication, there is support from the community. This support takes the form of tacit acceptance of the functioning of the organisation and the provision of labour to the organisation.[33] Research carried out in 2002 has indicated that 30 per cent of the UK public has boycotted a product or company for ethical reasons in the previous year.[34] This means that organisations have to take into account what the community and the public think are important and integrate this into their actions. It has been suggested that communities have become more important rather than less important.[35]

Relationships with communities have to be built on a continuous basis, and cannot be left to deteriorate and only get attention when the organisation wants something from the community.[36] This is seen in the 'think globally, act locally' philosophy of organisations.[37]

7.6.4 Government, Local Authorities and Regulatory Bodies

This refers to bodies that are created to oversee the activities of the organisation and affect organisations in geographical areas or within an economic area (such as the European Union or the Southern African Development Community).[38]

This group of stakeholders affects all organisations to a varying extent. All organisations are required to pay their taxes and are affected by the actions of the local authorities. However, not all industries have regulatory bodies that affect their operation.

An example of a regulatory influence can be seen in the communication industry. ICASA (the Independent Communication Authority of South Africa) has been created to regulate the telecommunication and broadcasting industries to the benefit of the public.[39] ICASA's mandate is based on the policy of the government to provide access to basic communications to all people in the country at an affordable price. ICASA's task thus includes licensing radio stations, enforcing compliance regulations and managing telecommunication frequencies. Service providers such as Telkom are required to get ICASA's permission to change their prices, as this affects accessibility to the service.

7.6.5 Press/Media

The media in their various forms are vitally important to an organisation with respect to how the organisation communicates with the general public and the community. The media are a powerful tool when an organisation is attempting to build public opinion, and can affect the reputation of the organisation among the members of the public.

Establishing a good relationship with the press and media representatives can be done by the organisation itself (and specifically the public relations practitioners), or it can use an external PR firm to build these relationships. Which method the organisation uses depends on its specific requirements, as both can provide an advantage to an organisation. In general, building relationships with the media and their representatives is similar to building relationships with other stakeholders, as discussed below.

7.7 Stages in Stakeholder Relationships

It has been proposed that there are three stages in the development of stakeholder relationships.[40] These stages are illustrated in figure 7.2.

Figure 7.2 Stages in Stakeholder Development[41]

It is necessary to examine each of these stages in more detail. It must be borne in mind that an organisation can be at a different stage of development with different stakeholder groups, depending on the relationship-building activities that have taken place in the past.

Stage 1: Stakeholder engagement

Engagement refers to the activity of opening the communication and interaction with a specific stakeholder. Part of this engagement activity involves an audit that the organisation conducts among each group of stakeholders so that it can identify the key issues associated with each stakeholder group.[42] This engagement will allow both parties to share ideas and opinions while exchanging views, and therefore allows for the development of a relationship. This is done through the creation of stakeholder councils and advisory boards.

Stage 2: Stakeholder satisfaction

Satisfaction comes about when the needs of the parties are met, and stakeholder satisfaction implies that the stakeholders feel that their needs are being met by the organisation. Should they not be satisfied, they will withdraw their support. Stakeholder satisfaction can be measured by using satisfaction studies (as discussed in chapter 3).[43]

Stage 3: Stakeholder retention

Retention is the organisation's ability to 'keep' its stakeholders as important contributors to the functioning of the organisation and the management of its various activities. Retention will allow for the creation of mutual value in the long term, to the benefit of both groups.

7.8   Strategies for Stakeholder Relationships

As has been indicated, lateral partnerships have an important effect on the relationship marketing strategy of the organisation. The question that can be posed is: What strategies can be used in the management of these relationships?

Communication is regarded as critical in building relationships with stakeholders. This group is large, making the use of mass media (as in the case of advertising) necessary.[44] In reaching these stakeholder groups, it has been suggested that the cost-effectiveness of the medium that is chosen is key. While advertising does contribute to the perceptions and reputation of the organisation, public relations activities can be regarded as the most suitable method.[45] Irrespective of the specific method selected by a particular organisation, the integration of this communication activity is essential in order to ensure that a consistent message is delivered to the stakeholders.

The Internet has changed the way in which organisations communicate with people and communities. If they do not communicate themselves, the public communicate with each other and develop campaigns using the Internet to organise their activities.[46]

As has already been discussed, relationships develop when both sides 'win' in that both sides gain from the relationship. In the past, organisations have decided on a course of action, informed the stakeholders about what they were going to do, and then defended their actions with question-and-answer sessions. This has not worked effectively and this approach has been re-examined. A new approach that has been developed is the Issues Negotiation™ approach.

The Issues Negotiation™ approach works through five stages, as follows:

Stage 1: Insight. Here the organisation seeks to understand the motivation of a particular stakeholder group. Without understanding the group's motivation, the organisation cannot effectively communicate with its members.

Stage 2: Include. The focus of this stage is to include all the stakeholders in the decision, and this may include inviting opponents of a particular project to take part, as well as friends.

Stage 3: Explore. This means that both groups explore the various alternatives and the assumptions on which they are based. Understanding a specific groups' perceptions means that the quality of the communication to them can improve, which contributes to the positive relationships that develop.

Stage 4: Negotiate. The purpose of negotiation is to find common ground. This may involve doing fact finding so that the issues can be correctly identified. It could be said that organisations should not make information available if it could be damaging to the organisation. However, previous situations have shown that keeping information out of the public eye does not improve the organisation's position, and, in fact, often it weakens it.

An example of an industry that has suffered from failing to make information available to the public is the cigarette industry. Initially it denied that cigarettes were dangerous, and even presented scientific information that 'proved' that smoking was good for you.[47] Later research has clearly indicated that smoking isn't 'good for you', and this has resulted in a number of court cases and huge damages being awarded against the tobacco industry in court.

Stage 5: Progress. Progress will be reflected in the plan that the parties compile to reflect the decisions and actions of the organisation. At this stage, understanding has developed and continuous communication and growth in understanding has meant that the relationship has continued to develop.

7.9   Summary

The focus of this chapter has been the stakeholders who are interested in the outcomes of the organisation. The concept of 'lateral partnerships' was identified and the individual components of this group of partners were examined. From this examination, it can be seen that relationship building with these partners requires an integrated approach among the various parts of the organisation. We have also seen that not all the stakeholders are equally important to all organisations, yet an organisation is required to build relationships with all these stakeholders in order to ensure its survival.

Discussion Questions

1.   What is meant by the term 'stakeholder'?
2.   Why is a stakeholder important to the organisation?
3.   Why could it be said that stakeholders are 'strategically significant'?
4.   What is meant by the triple bottom line? Why is it important to the organisation?
5.   What specific groups of stakeholders can be identified? What are their expectations of the organisation?
6.   What is the role of the shareholder in the functioning of the organisation?
7.   Comment on the specific target markets for the investor relations (IR) of the organisation.
8.   Are environmental shareholders equally important for all organisations? Give reasons for your answer.
9.   Comment on the influence that environmental shareholders are able to have on the organisation.
10. How do communities affect the functioning of the organisation?
11. Comment on the effect on the organisation of the press (or media) as a stakeholder.
12. A number of stages have been identified in the development of stakeholder relationships. Explain these three stages.

13. What specific strategies can an organisation use to build relationships with its stakeholders?

Mini Case Study[48, 49]

Ask any South African about a leading chemical organisation that manufactures petrol (fuel) and chemicals, and who has a major strategic effect on the South African economy, and Sasol's name will be mentioned. It is an organisation that affects all South Africans and the products they use, from the petrol in their car's fuel tank to the containers in which their favourite ice cream is sold.

Sasol was founded in 1950 and is today an integrated oil and gas company with substantial chemical interests. Perhaps it is most widely known for its oil-from-coal technology, which has placed it on the map. It not only manufactures products in South Africa, but also produces oil in Gabon and natural gas in Mozambique, and runs a gas-to-liquids project in Qatar.

Sasol's vision

Sasol's vision is as follows: 'To be a respected global enterprise, harnessing our talents in applying unique, innovative and competitive technologies to excel in selected markets in the energy and chemical sectors in Southern Africa and worldwide.'

The values that are encapsulated in this vision are those of a customer focus, 'winning with people' (expressed in the company's encouragement of individual employees to develop their skills), safety, excellence 'in all we do', continuous improvement and integrity. All of these values describe how Sasol does business and how its operations are directed. Further, the Sasol brand is presented as being

- *Alive* (dynamic and inspiring)
- *Adventurous* (innovative and ambitious)
- *Always* (dedicated and reliable).

The nature of Sasol's business

But who or what exactly is Sasol? Sasol has seven key operating companies, and these reflect the nature of its business, namely:

- Sasol Chemical Industries Ltd

- Sasol Oil (Pty) Ltd

- Sasol Mining (Pty) Ltd

- Sasol Gas Holdings (Pty) Ltd

- Sasol Synfuels (Pty) Ltd

- Sasol Technology (Pty) Ltd

- Sasol Financing (Pty) Ltd.

There are three main business areas in which Sasol makes products:

- **Oil and gas business:** petrol and diesel, jet fuel, paraffin, gas, lubricants, bitumen, pipeline gas and chemical feedstock

- **Chemical business:** paints and coatings, perfumes and deodorants, pharmaceuticals, digital discs, footwear, automotive components, plastic film and packaging

- **Other chemical business:** household cleaning liquids, agricultural fertilisers, explosives for mining and quarrying, drilling fluids, polishes and coatings, anti-sunburn creams and water-treatment chemicals.

Customers

Sasol has the challenge of selling products to both business and individual consumers. Business consumers are the primary consumers of Sasol's products. Reading the list of products above, it can be seen that Sasol has a wide variety of B2B customers.

Employees

With the current situation in South African and the importance of skills to Sasol, a focus has been placed on having a well-trained and well-motivated workforce. Further, with the nature of Sasol's business, safety is one of the core values of the organisation. One of the main focus areas for the company is the training of current employees, while also being an employer of choice among graduates. The focus in Sasol is also ensuring that employees are fairly remunerated and keeping communication channels open in the organisation.

Shareholders

Sasol is listed on the JSE, as well as on the New York Securities Exchange. The company's major shareholders include the PIC Equities (10.8 per cent), Old Mutual Asset Managers (8.1 per cent) and Stanlib Ltd (4.4 per cent). Sasol's market capitalisation was estimated at more than R161 billion as at 31 December 2006. For the six months ending December 2006, the company's operating profit was R12.2 billion (which was 12 per cent higher than the previous period).

Regulatory and government authorities

'If a government thinks you are doing more harm than good, you won't be able to do business', so says Mike Rose from Sasol. This shows how important the government is in the functioning of business. It has been proposed that Sasol be taxed on its profits that resulted from the sudden surge in the oil price that started in late 2007 — a so-called windfall tax. A task team set up by the National Treasury made this tax proposal. In August 2007 it was decided that this tax would not be implemented, which, naturally, pleased Sasol.

Environmental stakeholders

Manufacturing the type of products that Sasol does creates the possibility that environmental damage will result from their manufacturing processes. To prevent this and make sure that it doesn't happen, Sasol has an extensive focus on health and safety. Reporting on the TBL is regarded as critical by the company.

Questions

1. Do you think lateral stakeholders are important to Sasol?
2. What do you think would happen to Sasol if it ignored its lateral partners?
3. Do you think it is possible to identify a 'most important stakeholder' in the case of Sasol? If so, whom would you identify? Motivate your answer clearly.
4. How does the international nature of Sasol's business impact on its relationship with its stakeholders?
5. What specific challenges does Sasol face with respect to its shareholders?
6. Do you think its environmental stakeholders would be different if Sasol were based in a European country? What pressure is placed on Sasol with regard to environmental issues?

7. What effect does the government (specifically in South Africa) have on Sasol as an organisation?

References

1   Polonsky, MJ & Scott, D. 2005. An empirical examination of the stakeholder strategy matrix. *European Journal of Marketing*, 39 (9/10), p. 1200.
2   Lynch, R. 2000. *Corporate Strategy.* Harlow: Prentice-Hall, p. 520.
3   Christopher, M, Payne, A & Ballantyne, D. 2002. *Relationship Marketing: Creating Stakeholder Value.* Oxford: Butterworth-Heinemann, p. 77.
4   *Ibid.*, p. 80.
5   Morgan, RM & Hunt, SD. 1994. The commitment-trust theory of relationship marketing. *Journal of Marketing*, 58 (3), pp. 20–38.
6   Christopher *et al., op. cit.*, p. 80.
7   Morgan & Hunt, *op. cit.*, p. 21.
8   Pile, J. 2002. A new bottom line for companies. *Financial Mail*, 22 March. <http://secure.financialmail.co.za/02/0322/focus/afocus.htm>, accessed 22 August 2007.
9   Williams, *op. cit.*
10 *Ibid.*
11 *Ibid.*
12 Pile, *op. cit.*
13 Williams, *op. cit.*
14 *Ibid.*
15 *Ibid.*
16 Dekker, C. 2004. Summary of the King Report by Cliffe Dekker Attorneys. <http://www.mbendi.com/cliffedekker/literature/corpgov/>, accessed 22 August 2007.
17 Titi, F, Sowazi, N & Adomakoh, D. 2005. Digging deeper into BEE. *Financial Mail*, 18 March. <http://secure.financialmail.co.za/05/0318/opinion/guest.htm>, accessed 28 September 2007.
18 Republic of South Africa. Department of Trade and Industry. 1998. BBBEE Bill, Act 55. <http://www.dti.gov.za/bee/beebill.pdf>, accessed 22 August 2007.
19 Lynch, *op. cit.*, p. 521.
20 Peck *et al., op. cit.*, p. 239.
21 Payne, A, Holt, S & Frow, P. 2000. Integrating employee, customers and shareholder value through an enterprise performance opportunity for financial services. *International Journal of Bank Marketing*, 18 (6), p. 262.
22 *Ibid.*, p. 261.
23 Lynch, *op. cit.*, p. 521.
24 Diamond, B. 1997. It's the bottom line, stupid — communication of investor relations. <http://www.findarticles.com/p/articles/mi_m4422/is_n5_v14/ai/_19537770/pg_2>, accessed 17 August 2007.
25 Buss, D. 2003. Branding your stock — investor relations — investor-relations pros use techniques from the advertising world. <http://www.findarticles.com/p/articles/mi_m3870/is_10_19/ai_106474419>, accessed 17 August 2007.

26 *Ibid.*

27 Hazelhurst, E. 2005. Get it wrong and face shareholders in court. *Financial Mail*, 29 April. <http://secure.financialmail.co.za/05/0429/business/bbus.htm>, accessed 20 August 2007.

28 McAlpine, R. 2004. Round one to the small guy. *Financial Mail*, 12 March. <http://secure.financialmail.co.za/04/0312/focus/ffocus.htm>, accessed 22 August 2007.

29 Diamond, *op. cit.*

30 Christopher *et al., op. cit.*, p. 99.

31 *Ibid.*

32 Pile, *op. cit.*

33 George, B. 2003. Managing stakeholder vs. responding to shareholders. *Strategy and Leadership*, 31 (6), pp. 36–40.

34 Watson, T, Osborne-Brown, S & Longhurst, M. 2002. Issues Negotiation™: Investing in stakeholders. *Corporate Communications: An International Journal*, 7 (1), p. 55.

35 George, *op. cit.*

36 *Ibid.*

37 *Ibid.*

38 Christopher *et al., op. cit.*, p. 100.

39 Anonymous. 2007. <http://www.icasa.org.za/content.aspx?Page=17>, accessed 17 August 2007.

40 Payne *et al., op. cit.*, p. 259.

41 *Ibid.*

42 Payne, A, Ballantyne S & Christopher, M. 2004. A stakeholder approach to relationship marketing strategy. *European Journal of Marketing*, 39 (7/8), p. 864.

43 *Ibid.*, p. 866.

44 Lynch *op. cit.*, p. 219.

45 *Ibid.*, p. 221.

46 Watson *et al., op. cit.*, p. 55.

47 *Ibid.*, p. 60.

48 Sasol. 2007. *Sasol Facts.* Corporate publication of Sasol Ltd.

49 Williams, *op. cit.*

CHAPTER

8

Planning a CRM Strategy

Learning Outcomes

After studying this chapter, you should be able to:

- identify the factors determining the success of a CRM initiative

- explain, with the aid of practical examples, each stage in the CRM planning process

- apply the stages in the CRM planning process to a practical situation.

8.1 Introduction

Many organisations expect CRM initiatives to accomplish a lot, but few put the customer first or measure the effect of CRM from a customer perspective. Instead, they focus primarily on internal measurements such as return on investment (ROI) and market share, and on improving efficiency.

> ### Too few companies are putting customers first[1]
>
> One-fifth of the top global 3 500 organisations have implemented CRM. More than $150 billion had been spent on CRM-enabling technologies by 2004, and most of this was wasted, says international research company the Gartner Group. It says that during that period, 55 per cent of CRM initiatives did not meet measurable benefit objectives or achieve effective return on investment.

Lack of planning, undefined business goals and the absence of measurement are most often the reasons for CRM failure. CRM is not just about technology – it is a holistic approach to refocusing the business on customers, rather than on the internal structure of the organisation. It is more about the competencies that an organisation has, rather than a list of technologies, the goal being to win, get to know and keep profitable customers.

In South Africa over the past few years, the first wave of CRM has focused on implementing technology solutions and improving efficiency. However, business-focused CRM involves putting customers first – taking a fresh look at how customers are dealt with; finding out about, and solving, commercial problems; and changing the culture of the organisation as a whole to serve customers more effectively and profitably.

Management planning and decision making are vital to co-ordinate the direction and resource allocation of any organisation, and are important factors in creating the organisational climate in which relationships can flourish.[2] What CRM management does *not* imply is a formula or prescriptive solution that can guarantee success. Both the decision to apply relational strategies and the ways in which these are designed and implemented are, if they are to be successful, situation specific. There are thus no specific, generally applicable guidelines for CRM to be successful. An organisation may use a relational approach for some customers who require this. Other customers may not seek such services, or may contribute nothing to profit. The skill of the marketer is not in the application of CRM strategies as such, but in *applying the strategies to appropriate customers in given situations.*

Grönroos, one of the founders of relationship marketing says:

> We know too little about how relationship marketing should be integrated best into the planning of a company. The only way to find out is through trial and error, and through research. Under these circumstances, it seems reasonable to start by adding CRM dimensions to the marketing plan in use, retaining its basic format.[3]

This chapter focuses on planning a CRM strategy. We deal firstly with some factors influencing the success of CRM. Then guidelines or processes for planning for CRM will be suggested, which includes the development of CRM strategies to improve customer loyalty.

8.2 Factors Determining CRM Success

For organisations to meet the challenge of a relationship approach means having a culture of customer orientation, and the staff resources (this includes their recruitment, training, remuneration, number and control), system resources (i.e. structures, procedures and priorities) and information resources to effectively implement the relationship approach. This also means understanding the classic relationship between an organisation and its customers, as well as their product needs, interaction modes and profitability over time. We referred to all these important factors in chapter 1, section 1.5.

The question may be asked: 'How does an organisation create a customer-centric business philosophy and culture?' To successfully implement CRM in an organisation, there should first of all be a commitment from top or senior management.[4]

8.2.1 Customer-centricity

Customer-centricity requires a focus on the central role of the customer, whereas in the past, the focus may have been on marketing strategies designed to promote the sales of specific products or services.

The main implementation barriers that an organisation that wishes to implement CRM will face are not those raised by customers or others in the value chain, but by senior staff members within the organisation itself. Before senior management will commit to changing those strategies that have previously made the organisation successful, the linkage between CRM and shareholder value creation will need to be clearly demonstrated. In addition to calculating the financial value of introducing CRM as an aid to mustering support for the initiative among the organisation's financial and other managers, prospective CRM managers can experience additional challenges, such as:[5]

- finding the best CRM examples to benchmark their project against in this emerging area where few suppliers have developed fully integrated CRM initiatives that have effectively planned the introduction of the most effective CRM system;
- envisioning the end state of CRM, and the investments and actions needed to achieve this end state;
- focusing on working with core customers to develop the transition plan from the existing relationship to the desired one – a particularly daunting challenge;
- determining how to really add value to core customers, and doing this faster than competitors; and
- demonstrating the feasibility of the CRM concept by using pilot tests to demonstrate the effectiveness of the proposed CRM system prior to rolling it out.

Many CEOs talk of relationships quite separately from the other aspects of their business, and have no formal plan for advancing the customer relationship and deepening bonding. Being 'nice' and helping the customer do not, in themselves, constitute a relationship. Rather, relationships can and should be specifically planned.[6] And if top management begins to understand the full importance of the customer relationship through this planning process, it will start to place the relationship at the centre of the business, and link its various strategies and capabilities to improving relationships with all stakeholders. CRM cannot simply be added onto marketing, with business otherwise proceeding as before; CRM has organisation-wide implications.

In order to compete effectively in an uncertain business environment, many CEOs hope that CRM will be a 'cure'. However, up to 80 per cent of all CRM initiatives fail to deliver on their promises. The main reason for this failure is not CRM itself, but lack of planning, and the absence of clear goals and strategies. If implemented correctly, CRM can offer many benefits in less than three months.[7]

As mentioned earlier, CRM is an organisation-wide issue, and the role of all employees is of critical importance. Management should create, continuously encourage, and improve its understanding of and appreciation for the roles of the employees in the organisation. Employees should have holistic views of their jobs, and have the optimum mix of skills, knowledge and personal traits that contact personnel in particular need in order to implement CRM. They must be prepared (through training) both in terms of knowledge and skills if the organisation expects to earn loyalty by helping clients make wiser purchase decisions than they might make at competing organisations. Monitoring staff performance and rewarding staff competence are also important factors in ensuring excellent service.

Developing a service culture is a means of creating and enhancing good interactive marketing performance needed for implementing a relationship marketing strategy. The employees involved in marketing have been called 'part-time' marketers. They have to learn to perform their tasks in a marketing-like way so that the customers will want to return.

8.2.2 System Resources

The success of CRM is heavily dependent upon the alignment and integration of all related business processes. The integration of the different departments within an organisation can make the difference between the success or failure of a CRM initiative. For example, while many successful companies have automated their front- and back-office and supply-chain systems, they will still need an extra information system to tie them all together.

If the organisation wants to develop better relationships with its more profitable customers, it needs to first revamp the key business processes that relate to customers, from customer service to order fulfillment. A CRM rollout will succeed only after the organisation and its processes have been restructured in order to better meet customer needs.

8.2.3 Information Resources

Two important information resources are *customer information and knowledge*, and *acquiring a CRM software system*.

Customer information and knowledge

It was pointed out in chapter 1 that information about customers is of paramount importance to CRM. Information on the organisation's existing customers will form the core of customer data. The specific information held may vary by type of market. For example, a sophisticated consumer data system may use the postal code to differentiate specialist geo-demographic data or include lifestyle information that allows customer profiles to be developed.

Customer information is potentially an invaluable aid in decision making. Moreover, the information collected for marketing purposes must, like the marketing function itself, be future-oriented. It must be possible to exploit customer data to drive future marketing programmes, and the data provides the basis of a strategy to do this.

This brings us to the important issue of implementing a CRM software system.

CRM technology

The success of any CRM initiative depends largely on ensuring that the most appropriate facilitator with regard to CRM technology has been selected to assist the organisation in utilising CRM successfully. The system must be flexible and easy to customise, be available for individual or concurrent users, permit future functionality without additional modules having to be purchased, and require a low level of expertise to maintain it, especially if maintenance is to be carried out internally.

Too many companies underestimate the comprehensive changes required to achieve truly profitable customer relationships, and become disappointed when their initiatives fail to deliver. For example, after spending $7.8 billion on the CRM technology market in 1999, companies were subsequently still experiencing margin erosion, customer defections and declining market share. The simple truth is that the reason so many CRM initiatives fall short of expectations is because the focus has been almost exclusively on installing a technological 'silver bullet'.[8] Technology implementation, in and of itself, is not a solution with tangible rewards. Like training or process design, technology is one of many tools that enable an organisation to become customer-centric. Those companies that have been successful with CRM initiatives have been successful by understanding the complete definition of CRM and by implementing a solution that builds and maintains the company's momentum. These companies realise that technology, though important, must be accompanied by changes in the organisation itself.

Technology is not necessarily required for effective CRM

Consider a successful small business. The business owner and the staff work hard to provide personal, high-quality service, thus building a loyal customer base over time. Computers are not necessarily required for them to do this.[9]

As the pyramid diagram in figure 8.1 shows, CRM must start with a business strategy that drives changes in the organisation and its work processes, which are, in turn, enabled by information technology. The reverse does not work — a company cannot automate its way to a new business strategy. In fact, the majority of projects that focus on technology first, rather than business objectives, are destined for failure, according to extensive best-practices research. However, a customer-centric business can reap significant benefits using CRM technology.

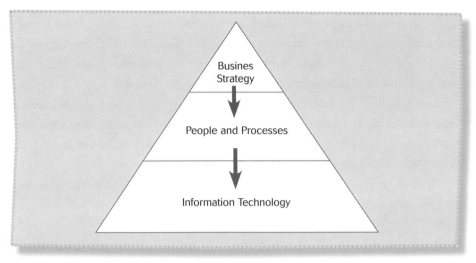

Figure 8.1 CRM Is More than Just Software[10]

Successful CRM initiatives start with a business strategy and philosophy that aligns company activities around customer needs. CRM technology is a critical enabler of the processes required to turn strategy into business results.

Integrating customer data[11]

It is necessary to link all sales and servicing departments and the front office through to back-office systems where a great deal of the information about customers and the history of their interactions is stored and updated. This linking is essential to deliver the right information to the right person at the right time in order to ensure that adequate support is provided to a particular client so as to maximise the value of the interaction for both parties. Linking the front and back offices is all about integrating the data from different parts of the organisation to ensure that all pertinent information about that particular client and his or her importance to the organisation is accessible at the right point, is understood and is in a format that can be used both easily and effectively.

The organisation needs to integrate every single interaction it has with the customer, whether it is a call to its call centre or a request via the Internet. These interactions also require interfacing with back-office systems such as central billing and data on products and services, as well as with all elements of the supply chain.

A CRM system must be capable of transforming all knowledge about key customers into valuable business intelligence in real time through any channel. Through

CRM processes, an organisation can synchronise its systems around service delivery to the customer rather than just synchronising data around itself. Then it will be able to understand and predict customer behaviour, implement smarter customer strategies, and maximise its own and its customers' profitability.

The quality of the data used in successful CRM applications is also critical. Corporate CRM systems fail because they provide reams of sales operational data that, in itself, is meaningless. These front-office systems must be integrated with analytical solutions that convert this operational data into real business intelligence.

A business must actually plan how it will create, implement and manage a programme to ensure the building of relationships with its customers.[12]

8.3　The CRM Planning Process

CRM offers organisations the opportunity to build long-term customer relationships and to regard these relationships as a key marketing asset within the organisation. In balancing the need to develop customer acquisition and retention strategies, organisations can improve their profitability as customer retention increases. For example, a small improvement in customer retention rates from 85 to 90 per cent

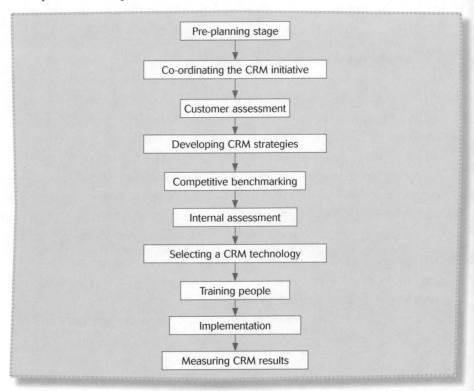

Figure 8.2 Stages in the CRM Planning Process

could result in net present value profits rising from 35 to 95 per cent among businesses.[13] The role of customer retention in developing CRM strategies is therefore critical.

A company wishing to improve relationships with its customers, thereby improving profitability, could employ the planning process illustrated in figure 8.2.

We will now look at each of the stages in the CRM planning process.

8.3.1 Pre-planning Stage

This is essentially a planning stage before the actual process begins. It is aimed at providing management with justification for the expenditure of time and effort, and outlining the various components necessary to ensure that the initiative delivers to management's expectations.[14]

An organisation must have a clear understanding of why CRM is needed –what the underlying platform, compelling vision and critical goals are to justify undertaking this transformation. It should think about and document ideas on how a new CRM philosophy will improve the company's competitiveness. Realistic goals and expectations need to be set and anticipated results considered.[15] Furthermore, the organisation should recognise that, while the greatest return from a CRM investment will be long term in nature, there are numerous short-term benefits as well. For example:

> **Short-term benefits of CRM**
>
> CRM can provide immediate 'cheap growth' just by uncovering opportunities to re-allocate sales resources from customers who are less likely to buy to those who are more likely to buy.[16]

These CRM vision and goals must have champions at all levels of the organisation, from senior management to frontline customer contacts. The sooner this support is secured and communicated, the better the opportunity for success. Project champions will play a vital role in day-to-day guidance and decision making, and will act as referees when needed.

It is also necessary to reconcile the magnitude of the coming change with the organisation's readiness. If the company does not have the depth or breadth of resources for this transition, it is best to secure external resources required for CRM implementation early on, and certainly before the project begins. The number and type of resources needed to achieve success must not be underestimated.

8.3.2 Co-ordinating the CRM Initiative

The most efficient and effective way to co-ordinate and execute the many tasks required to embed CRM into an organisation's culture is to treat the transition as a project. It is important to appoint a project manager to lead the CRM change, one who is accountable for achieving measurable results. The more senior and respected this person is in the organisation, the better. The project manager will need to assemble a multidiscipline implementation team, including representatives from each department involved in the transition. This core team should be kept small and agile, and it should be supplemented as each development cycle dictates. Additional team members could include marketing leaders, functional and technical team leaders, analysts, developers, technical architects, database administrators, trainers, and field sales and support personnel.[17]

It is advisable that, in addition to this, a steering committee of senior executives be formed that can provide expertise and guidance throughout the CRM transformation. By means of consistent communications and involvement with a larger group, momentum can be built and maintained throughout the organisation.

A detailed, precise project plan and time line is also required. Since the CRM implementation process will involve multiple development cycles, an overall road map that illustrates how each cycle fits within the overall plan should be created. A step-by-step, phased approach, establishing tangible milestones and metrics along the way, must be followed. Each project or department should have measurable short-term goals, as well as a long-term vision for the whole organisation. An organisation should be careful, however, not to let the plan dominate the planning. There will be unanticipated roadblocks and tasks that will necessitate adjustments being made.

Finally, clear roles and responsibilities must be established for each team member, based on the project plan and goals, with the timing and the criteria for success being crystal clear.

8.3.3 Customer Assessment

This stage of the planning process looks at where the organisation is now with regard to its customers and relationship marketing. Every customer-centric organisation must define, or refine, its customer vision. What can the company provide for customers that meets their needs and, therefore, fosters loyal and profitable relationships? To answer this type of question, the organisation must listen to what customers have to say and think about the business from their perspective. This may require original customer research to understand fully how the customers view the company, its services, people and other capabilities, both in absolute terms and relative to competitors.

In customer assessment, the profitability of customers needs to be established. Customer profitability is largely dependent on customer satisfaction, customer retention and customer loyalty (these factors were discussed in chapter 2).

Customer satisfaction, retention and loyalty

Customer satisfaction is measured by the rate at which customers are kept — the customer retention rate. This is expressed as the percentage of customers at the beginning of the year that still remain at the end of the year. The more satisfied the customers are, the longer they stay and thus the higher the retention rate. A retention rate of 80 per cent means that, on average, customers remain loyal for five years, whereas one of 90 per cent pushes the average period of loyalty up to ten years. And as the average of 'life' of a customer increases, so does the profitability of that customer to the firm. So as the retention rate goes up, so too does overall profitability.

It pays to retain customers[18]

A cost study of service companies found that customer retention has a more powerful effect on profits than market share, scale economies and other variables that are usually associated with competitive advantage. More specifically, it was established that companies that reduce customer defections by 5 per cent can boost profits by between 25 per cent and 85 per cent.

The service companies have experienced profit increases of anything from 30 per cent to 125 per cent. This latter result was achieved by a financial services company that succeeded in increasing its retention rate from an industry average of 90 per cent to 95 per cent. Over a period of six years, its market position rose from 38th to fourth in its industry.

Measuring the profitability of customers[19]

Once a firm has recognised the importance of building customer relationships, it needs to decide which customers it wants to build closer relationships with in the future.

As companies move towards one-to-one marketing, they need to develop a longer-term view of the value of their customers. Effectively, relationship marketers need to predict the future purchasing behaviour of key customers to arrive at their customer lifetime value (CLV). CLV looks at what the retained customer is worth to the organisation now, based on the predicted future transactions and costs. All costs should be allocated to customers, including sales, marketing, finance, customer service and support, inventory-carrying and other costs not always attributed to specific customers.[20] This is the 'cost to serve' the customer.

Looking forward to the value of future purchases and costs, expressed as the present value of a stream of future profits, fits more comfortably with the development of a relationship marketing approach, which is concerned with unlocking value for the firm and its key customers.

To calculate the CLV, three sorts of information are needed:

- the anticipated lifetime of the customer relationship in months or years;
- the profit in each future period adjusted for any customer-specific capital costs, such as marketing and customised services; and
- a discount rate.

Revenue forecast ⟶ Cost forecast ⟶ Present value calculation ⟶ CLV
↑
Discount rate

CLV analysis suggests that the value of a relationship with a customer can be increased either by increasing the amount of profits (by increasing the revenue from the customer and/or decreasing costs to serve), or by extending the relationship lifetime. Customers at the beginning of their relationship lifetime will need a different CRM strategy to those approaching the declining stage of their relationship lifetime. Banks understand this principle well; they have identified students as potentially high value customers over a lifetime, even though in the short term they may be unprofitable. So, CLV calculations, often used to measure the profit impact of customer retention strategies, provide a better guide for customer strategy than the current period.

An accurate understanding of the value of customers' lifetime values can and will drive the successful management of companies in the foreseeable future.

The objective of customer selection is to detect and target customers based on their value. Customer selection strategies are applied when an organisation wants to target individual customers or groups of customers. The benefit of selecting the top 20 per cent of customers using a CLV score versus traditional metrics is that the average revenue for a customer selected on the basis of CLV is about 60 per cent greater than customers selected using other metrics.

New strategies to treat different customers differently need to be developed. This is the next logical step in the CRM planning process.

8.3.4 Developing CRM Strategies

In recent years, marketing managers have tried to measure and maximise the lifetime value of each and every customer. If a company truly understood each customer's lifetime value, it could maximise its own value by boosting the number, scope and duration of value-creating customer relationships. Some cutting-edge marketing strategies are available for maximising customer lifetime.[21] Each of these strategies plays a unique role in optimising shareholder value, customer equity and overall profitability. Each strategy also works in combination with other strategies to increase overall impact on the company's value.

To treat different customers differently, it is necessary to group them into value-based tiers; i.e. groups of customers with similar values to the organisation. In this

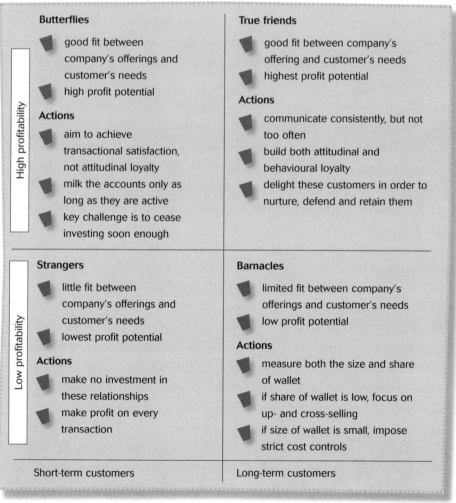

Figure 8.3 Selecting CRM Strategies

way, the most valuable customers, the ones that have the most potential to grow, as well as the unprofitable ones, can be identified. It is necessary to look at each group more closely, and profile its members by their needs and preferences.

Next, a specific set of strategies for retaining and growing the best customers must be defined. The organisation should recognise that these customers are the key to its success. On the other hand, cost-reduction strategies should be devised for the least profitable ones, or for customers who cost the company more than they contribute to it.

After analysing the customers' lifetime value or future profitability and the projected duration of their relationships, the organisation can place each of them into one of four categories, as shown in figure 8.3.[22] The four quadrants of the matrix suggest how customers can be sorted on the basis of customer longetivy and profitability for the firm. While there may be long-standing customers who are only marginally profitable, there may be short-term customers who are highly profitable. Hence, it becomes clear that the relationship between loyalty and profitability is by no means assured.

It should now become clear that when profitability and loyalty are considered at the same time, different customers need to be treated in different ways. Now, what kind of relationship management strategies should the organisation apply to the different segments? Management should assess which customers in an organisation's current customer base merit a continued relationship, and then size and align the organisation in accordance with the mix of customers on which the organisation has chosen to focus. It is also necessary to consider the current state of the relationship that the organisation has with each customer by measuring the quality of that relationship. Let us consider each of the segments in figure 8.3, and indicate what strategy would be appropriate for each segment.

Strangers

The strangers, as the name suggests, are the least profitable customers for the firm. For the customers who have no loyalty and bring in no profits — we call them 'strangers' — the answer is simple: identify them early and do not invest anything in them. Not all customers merit consideration by an organisation. Customers who are currently unprofitable will probably be unprofitable tomorrow and do not merit further investment. Not investing in these customers may have additional benefits for an organisation — it can improve the organisation's stock market valuation in an unexpected way if competitors take up former customers and become less profitable themselves as a result. Hence, every transaction with the strangers should be profitable.

Customers who do not provide much value to the firm (low CLV) but get large value from the firm may be considered 'free riders', i.e. they derive large benefits without providing much in return. In some cases, a firm may be better off either raising prices for these customers or for the resources devoted to them. Thus, more customers or a higher market share may not be necessarily good for a firm. Some companies recognise this and cut back the resources devoted to their low-value customers.[23]

It is, however, not easy to identify relationships, especially those that ought to be terminated.

> ### Role in banking relationships[24]
>
> In a study in the banking industry, for example, it was found that personal bankers can be effective in maintaining and enhancing relationships with customers allocated to them, but do not have a role in identifying and establishing relationships. Given that few bankers in the survey could accurately calculate relationship profitability, the task of identifying relationships that ought to be terminated cannot be undertaken by such bankers, also possibly due to lack of training in this field. This uninformed basis is not an appropriate one on which to make decisions about allocation of time, effort and resources.

For customers in the other three quadrants of the matrix, the choice of strategy will make a material difference to the segment's profitability.[25]

True friends

A 'soft' approach is more appropriate for profitable customers who are likely to be loyal — your 'true friends'. They are today's ideal customers — those who look as if they will be profitable in the future. Profitable, loyal customers are usually satisfied with existing arrangements.

True friends are the most valuable customers of all. They fit in well with the company offerings. They are also steady purchasers, buying regularly, but perhaps not intensively, over time. In managing these true friends, firms should provide consistent, yet intermittently spaced communications. Firms should strive to achieve attitudinal and behavioural loyalty among these customers.

In managing these true friends, the greatest trap is overkill. A mail-order company, for instance, found that intensifying the level of contact through, for example, increasing the number of mailings was more likely to put off a loyal and profitable customer than to increase sales. People flooded with mail may throw everything out without looking at it. Sent less mail, however, they are more likely to look at what

True friends

The mail-order company also found that the true friends tended to return goods at a relatively high rate, reflecting their comfort in engaging with the company's processes. They are also steady purchasers, buying regularly, but not intensively, over time.[26]

they get. Indeed, the mail-order company found that its profitable loyal customers were not among those who received the most mailings.

What is more important is that companies need to concentrate on finding ways to bring to the fore their true friends' feelings of loyalty, because 'true' believers are the most valuable customers of all.

Companies can do several things to make loyal customers feel rewarded for their loyalty, for example:

Reward loyal customers[27]

A supermarket chain lets its loyal customers opt in to e-mailings of special recipes, price promotions and so on. It also grants them preferred access to company-sponsored seasonal events. For example, they get exclusive early access to semi-annual week-long wine festivals in which they have the opportunity to buy many of the better wines that are only available in limited quantities. Such measures are already having an appreciable impact on the purchasing volumes and profitability of loyal customers.

Butterflies

These customers are profitable but 'un-loyal'. However, although staying for only a short term, they offer high profitability for the company. They enjoy finding out the best deals, and avoid building a stable relationship with any single provider. So companies should stop investing in these customers once their buying activity drops. They could become less profitable or even unprofitable in the future. The challenge in managing these customers is to milk them for as much as you can for the short time they are buying from you. The classic mistake made in managing these accounts is continuing to invest in them after their buying activity drops off. Research shows that attempts to convert butterflies into loyal customers are seldom successful.[28] Instead of treating butterflies as potential true believers, therefore, managers should look for ways to enjoy them while they can and find the right moment to stop investing in them. In practice, this usually means a short-term hard sell through promotions and mailing blitzes that include special offers on other products, an approach that might well irritate loyal customers. One could telephone those identified as butterflies four or five times shortly after their most recent purchase and follow up with just one direct mailing six to 12 months later, depending on the product category. If these communications bear no fruit, the company should drop contact altogether.

Some of these customers may, however, be made profitable and should not be ignored.[29] Give them strategic attention and ongoing opportunities to create mutual value that will enhance prospects for both the organisation and the customers, so that the relationship will remain profitable and even result in rewards in the future.

Barnacles

Barnacles are those customers who, in spite of being long-term customers, offer low profitability for the firm, and thus do not generate satisfactory return on investments due to their small size and low volume of transactions. These customers are the most problematic and, like barnacles on the hull of a cargo ship, they only create additional drag, thus 'dragging' the organisation down. Between 30 to 40 per cent of a company's revenue base is generated by customers who, on a stand-alone basis, are not profitable, because the size and volume of their transactions are too low. Properly managed, though, they can sometimes become profitable.

The first step is to determine whether the problem is a small wallet (i.e. the customers are not valuable to begin with and are not worth chasing), or a small share of the wallet (i.e. they could spend more and should be chased). Some grocery chains do it rather well. By looking closely at data on the type and number of products that individuals purchase (e.g. baby or pet food), such a company can derive amazingly reliable estimates of the size and share of the individual customers' wallets it has already captured in each product category. Then it can easily distinguish which loyal customers are potentially profitable and offer them products associated with those already purchased, as well as certain other items in seemingly related categories.

Barnacles disciplined

Banks, for example, prefer the average customer to use automated teller machines (ATMs) for routine transactions. If banks must maintain teller service for customers, the benefits of the technologies and processes in which they have invested will not be realised. They therefore charge customers for teller services for routine transactions. Their customers are being 'disciplined' financially to encourage them to use the ATM in future.

These barnacles could also be disciplined, by charging customers in this segment a fee for not conforming to the organisation's 'rules of engagement' as 'best customers'.[30]

There is no one right way to make loyalty profitable. Different approaches will be more suited to different businesses, depending on the profiles of their customers and the complexity of their distribution channels. But whatever the context, no company should ever take for granted the idea that managing customers for loyalty is the same as managing them for profits. The only way to strengthen the link between profits and loyalty is to manage both at the same time. Fortunately, technology is making that task easier every day, allowing companies to record and analyse the often complex and sometimes even perverse behaviour of their customers.

Let us now continue with the CRM planning process.

8.3.5 Competitive Benchmarking[31]

Competitive benchmarking means investigating competitors' actions with regard to relationships and their customers. The idea is to establish how the competition relates to CRM. Moreover, benchmarking refers to a comparison with the very best — not the average or the mediocre. It requires comparison, not only with competitors, but with best practice in whatever company or industry can be found. But, because the battle in the marketplace is for 'share of mind', it is customers' perceptions that must be measured.[32]

The measures that can be used in this type of benchmarking programme include delivery reliability, ease of ordering, after-sales service, the quality of sales representation, and the accuracy of invoices and other documentation. These measures are not chosen at random, but are selected because of their importance to the customer. Market research, often based on in-depth interviews, would typically be employed to identify what these key success factors are. The elements that customers identify as being the most important, then, form the basis for the benchmark questionnaire.

One way to assess competitors' CRM prowess is to become a customer of the competitor.[33] This will allow you to observe selected key processes first hand, even though you will likely not be seen by the competitor as a core customer. Or, to assess production processes and to render a judgement on flexibility, you may wish to buy your competitors' products and tear them apart to see what they are supplying to their customers.

It may also be necessary to examine the CRM capabilities and processes of companies in similar industries, perhaps internationally. This can give you some of the information needed to develop cutting-edge CRM, without regard to current industry practice.

> **Tear competitors' products apart**[34]
>
> General Motors has a 'vehicle assessment centre' to dismantle and lay out the contents of up to 15 new cars a year for 19 000 engineers, designers and managers to examine.

In addition to comparing the value of your company in the minds of customers relative to competitors, it is appropriate to ask questions such as:

- How have competitors been able to achieve this position?
- What can we learn from them?
- What are their strategies concerning CRM and more generally?
- Can we target their customers or distribution channel intermediaries for transfer to our business?

8.3.6 Internal Assessment

A company also needs to take a close look at itself to determine what kinds of relationships it is most suited to, and even whether CRM is appropriate for it.

Is CRM appropriate?

One of the key issues in the internal assessment is an understanding of the core business in which the company is engaged. Thus, a company must ask itself whether it, in fact, should focus on the needs of individual customers or not. In certain types of business, it would be more profitable to focus on mass production and mass service.

Business culture

In order to implement CRM successfully, a crucial requirement is that the culture of the business must emphasise self-respect, respect for others, and a commitment to mutual and active listening. If these are lacking, then the culture needs to be re-formed before proceeding with the CRM project. And in this process, the initiative needs to come from top management.

Top management support

The CRM initiative needs to be supported by top management (as stated in chapter 1). If, for example, top management is incapable of forming relationships, then no meaningful relationships will be formed.

Sometimes mass production is more profitable[35]

Some companies are in the business of producing high-volume goods at the lowest possible price, and CRM will distract such a company from its single-minded focus on being the low-cost producer in its industry. Yet even for this company, CRM may still have an important role, such as in the company's relationship with distribution channel intermediaries.

In some industries, the lifetime profitability from individual customers is not high enough to warrant an all-out CRM effort. For example, supermarket chains secure a very modest return on sales, usually less than two per cent. Here, the lifetime revenue potential of an individual customer and the costs of bonding to each one of them may be uneconomic for both the retailer and the consumer products company that produces a single brand or just a few products. In these situations, it may still pay the company to cater to market segments and local or regional market preferences, or focus on frequency marketing by providing inducements for the customer to shop at the store again or to repurchase the brand, rather than adopting CRM as a strategy.

Capable staff

Other aspects that need to be assessed are the company's members of staff, e.g. whether they possess the necessary skills and knowledge for CRM; the capabilities of the organisation, e.g. technologies and processes and their adaptability; and whether the company can afford to change its technologies and processes.

Processes

To be truly customer-centric and leverage the power of today's CRM systems, processes must be tailored to the customer experience. This is best accomplished by constructing a detailed customer touch map, which defines each interaction with the company along the customer life cycle. This will allow the organisation to understand the customer's entire experience, as is shown in figure 8.4.

The touch map will identify the areas of the customer experience that are going well, and where there is pain or confusion. For example, the basic touch map highlights the potential opportunity to streamline the survey process to improve the customer's experience. An organisation can begin automating the processes that are working well, but rethink those processes that may be damaging to the customer experience. One should begin by looking at the experiences of the most valued customers, then move to the ones who are the most likely to grow. When the pain points have been removed from these customers' experiences, then one can begin to re-engineer any inefficient back-office processes. The savings from the newly gained efficiency can be reinvested in the more profitable customers.

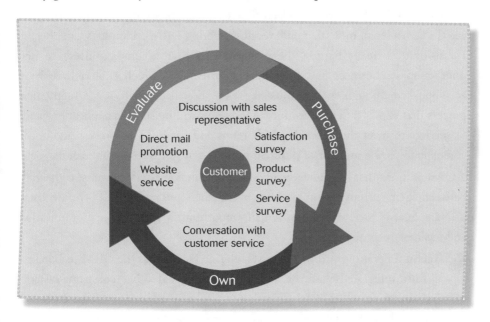

Figure 8.4 Customer Touch Map[36]

It is important to remember to review, and possibly re-engineer, channel processes, and evaluate their effectiveness and efficiency. One could work with end users to design and validate any process changes that need to be made. These processes then need to be translated into business and functional requirements, and ultimately business rules. Up to this point, the CRM-related work has been strategic and process oriented. With the strategy in place, the company is ready to fully leverage its enabling technologies.[37]

8.3.7 Selecting a CRM Technology

If an organisation is looking to select a CRM provider, it is necessary to first take a long and very analytical look at the organisation's own business processes, and to take an equally long and hard look at the organisational culture and, specifically, at all customer-facing management and staff. It is in these realms that success or failure of any CRM programme or project will be born. The astute organisation will discover rapidly that the greater part of CRM lies in people and processes. Only when these are aligned, streamlined and optimised will the organisation begin to gain a 'feel' for its own hybrid technology requirements; and only then will the 'right' CRM vendor, service provider or application begin to become apparent. CRM must, therefore, be a business-driven imperative, not a technology-driven exercise.[38]

For companies that have not selected a CRM technology, the process of navigating through a sea of more than 500 vendors offering CRM technology can be quite confusing.[39] To really harness the potential of CRM, a company needs to first understand its business and functional requirements, which should have been accomplished through the previous steps. The best decision tool is a methodical process that allows different vendors to bid on providing specific applications and/or services to meet the defined specifications and results. This process allows the company to view a number of different options and prices to accomplish its goals.

Organisations that have already invested in technology must now assess the gaps between their current technology usage and their full capacity. There are three primary areas to review for improvement opportunities: integration, customisation and business rules alignment.

- **Technology integration:** The first step is to ensure that the CRM technology is fully integrated with, or at least linked to, all other company systems containing customer data. One should also take advantage of the customer data held by channel partners and strategic alliances. All of these companies capture and maintain large amounts of data that helps identify customers and differentiates their value and needs.

- **Customisation:** To the extent that is feasible, the CRM applications should suit the way in which the affected employees work, and operate in ways that the company feels are a priority.

- **Business rules alignment:** Perhaps most importantly, CRM technology is only as effective as the processes and business rules behind it. With its customer strategies defined, the organisation's processes and business rules must be modified accordingly. The technology must support the company's customer vision and strategies, as well as any revised processes and business rules.

8.3.8 Training People

An organisation should never skimp on training; in other words, make sure that you train your people properly. This requires the organisation to plan ahead to allocate adequate time and funding to training. Typically, people require training in any new CRM business model, with its cultural shifts, processes and systems. Both job-level and executive training are required. An organisation should plan to spend 5 per cent of its total CRM investment on training.[40]

To test the effectiveness or relevancy of training, schedule regular audits of system usage, compliance with new processes and accurate data capture to ensure consistency and quality. If audits are not passed, additional training may be required. (Training is dealt with in chapter 9.)

8.3.9 Implementation

With proper planning and preparation for the CRM transformation, the organisation can begin implementation through distinct CRM development cycles. These cycles allow for a small, fast start, beginning with a controlled test or pilot group. The organisation should learn from the pilots, then refine the next implementation cycle and repeat the process as necessary.

In the beginning, one should not wait for perfection. The organisation will never be 100 per cent ready, so it should begin to roll out CRM at 80 per cent ready. It could implement in 10- to 12-week cycles and make corrections along the way. This is in fact a journey. (Implementation is dealt with in detail in chapter 9.)

8.3.10 Measuring CRM Results

Establishing appropriate, realistic metrics for assessing the effectiveness of CRM is extremely important. After all, the results determine whether CRM is perceived as succeeding or failing.[41]

One of the best ways to measure the CRM transformation is with a 'balanced' ROI scorecard. The balanced scorecard is a management tool consisting of a set of integrated performance measures that link current customers, internal processes, employees and systems performance to long-term financial success.[42] Put simply, a balanced scorecard includes financial measures that show the results of actions already taken.

The balanced scorecard incorporates both lag and lead indicators. Lag indicators could include revenue, market share, new product revenue and other classic financial factors. Lead indicators could include share of customers, revenue mix, customer satisfaction and the time spent with customers or customer involvement in product-planning cycles that show what is coming. A company should develop a CRM scorecard that incorporates measures for its priorities for all the solution components. It is also important to begin to quantify results as early as the first development cycle, using the most relevant data available.

Instead of quantitative measurements, one should consider, for example, what the ratio of customer profitability is to the number of calls made by telesales staff. One step further for measuring the ROI here is to differentiate service levels in conjunction with the number of calls or visits made, or the involvement of labour with a particular customer in relation to the customer's profitability.

8.4 Summary

In this chapter, we suggested broad guidelines for planning a CRM strategy. The factors determining CRM success were highlighted, and then the stages in a CRM planning process, including developing CRM strategies to treat different customers differently, were discussed.

Discussion Questions

1. Explain and illustrate the factors determining CRM success.
2. A company planning to implement customer relationship management needs advice on how to do this. Explain to the company each of the stages in the CRM planning process.
3. Before a CRM strategy is chosen for the different groups of customers, an organisation should determine their current and future profitability.
    (a) Explain the different customer segments that can be identified in this way.
    (b) Illustrate the different CRM strategies that could be used for each identified segment.

Mini Case Study[43]

Customer-based initiatives in the retail industry

Retailers have yet to fully leverage data to build customer relationships. Forty-five per cent of retailers do not have a data warehouse and cannot identify their best customers. The bulk of retailers' IT budgets has been spent on product-related systems, such as supply chain and inventory solutions.

Retailers have typically used the capabilities of new technology to improve efficiency, but have barely scratched the surface of improving effectiveness.

Efficiency is vital, but companies can hold onto customers more effectively by using data intelligently to identify and interact with their most valuable clients. Price becomes less important to customers if they have a good relationship with a company. It has been found that 60 per cent of those who do not have data warehouses would like to, and 100 per cent of survey participants plan to invest in retail CRM activities soon.

Questions

The above retailers have made important mistakes in their efforts in implementing CRM.

(a) Explain to the retailers the importance of a customer database.

(b) How would you advise the retailers on a planning process for CRM?

References

1 Coetzer, J. 2001. *Business Day*, 8 August, p. 8.
2 Egan, J. 2001. *Relationship Marketing*. Harlow: Pearson Education, p. 206.
3 Grönroos, C. 2000. The relationship marketing process: Interaction, communication dialogue value. Paper presented at the second WWW Conference on Relationship Marketing.
4 Greenberg, P. 2000. *CRM at the Speed of Light*. Berkeley: Osborne/McGraw-Hill, p. 36.
5 Brunjes, B & Roderick, R. 2002. Customer relationship management: Why it does and does not work in South Africa. Presentation at the IIMM Marketing Educators' Conference, 26–27 September, p. 9.
6 Gordon, IH. 1998. *Relationship Marketing*. Toronto: John Wiley, p. 135.
7 Peppers & Rogers Group. 2001. Damn the technology hurdles — full speed ahead! *White Paper*, p. 2.
8 *Ibid.*, p. 2.
9 Greenberg, *op. cit.*, p. 36.
10 *Ibid.*, p. 37.
11 Brunjes & Roderick, *op. cit.*
12 Brink, A & Machado, R. 1999. *Relationship Marketing*. Pretoria: Unisa, p. 4.
13 Ryals, LJ & Knox, S. 2006. Measuring risk-adjusted customer lifetime value and its impact on relationship marketing strategies and shareholder value. *European Journal of Marketing* 39 (5/6), pp. 456–58.
14 Gordon, *op. cit.*, p. 136.
15 Peppers & Rogers Group, *op. cit.*, p. 4.
16 <http://www.1to1.com>.
17 Peppers & Rogers Group, *op. cit.*, p. 5.
18 Payne, A & Frow, P. 2004. The role of mutichannel integration in customer relationship management. *Industrial Marketing Management*, pp. 527–38.
19 Based on Keiningham, TL, Aksoy, L & Bejou, D. 2006. <http://jrm.haworthpress.com>.
20 Gordon, *op. cit.*, p. 138.
21 Kumar, V. 2006. CLV: *The Databased Approach*. <http://jrm.haworthpress.com>.
22 Reinartz, W & Kumar, V. 2002. The mismanagement of customer loyalty. *Harvard Business Review*, p. 93.
23 Gupta, S & Lehmann, DR. 2006. *Customer Lifetime Value and Firm Valuation*. <http://jrm.haworthpress.com>.

24   Colgate, M & Stewart, K. 1998. The challenge of relationships in services: A New Zealand study. *International Journal of Service Industry Management*, 9 (5), pp. 454–68.

25   Based on Reinartz & Kumar, *op. cit.*, p. 93; Gordon, *op. cit.*, pp. 40–46.

26   Reinartz & Kumar, *op. cit.*, p. 94.

27   *Ibid.*, p. 93.

28   *Ibid.*, p. 94.

29   Gordon, *op. cit.*, p. 44.

30   Brink, A, Strydom, JW, Machado, R & Cant, MC. 2001. *Customer Relationship Management Principles*. Pretoria: Unisa, p. 58.

31   Gordon, *op. cit.*, pp. 138–41.

32   Hollensen, S. 2003. *Marketing Management: A Relationship Approach*. Harlow: *Financial Times*/Prentice-Hall, p. 89.

33   Gordon, *op. cit.*, p. 139.

34   *Ibid.*, p. 140.

35   *Ibid.*, p. 141.

36   Peppers & Rogers Group, *op. cit.*, p. 6.

37   *Ibid.*, p. 7.

38   Brink *et al.*, *op. cit.*, pp. 75–76.

39   <http://www.iq4hire.com>.

40   <http://www.computerworld.com>.

41   Peppers & Rogers Group, *op. cit.*, pp. 8–9.

42   Du Plessis, PJ, Jooste, CJ & Strydom, JW. 2001. *Applied Strategic Marketing*. Sandown: Heinemann, p. 424.

43   Peppers & Rogers Group, *op. cit.*

CHAPTER

9

Implementing CRM in an Organisation

Learning Outcomes

After studying this chapter, you should be able to:

- explain the importance of implementation for a CRM strategy
- explain three prerequisites for the implementation of any strategy
- explain why implementation is important for any strategy and the specific challenges in the case of a CRM strategy
- explain the term 'customer leader'
- explain the importance of technology in the implementation process
- explain the role of corporate culture in the implementation of a CRM strategy
- explain the importance of change management and resistance to change within an organisation
- explain the importance of control within the strategy implementation process, and specifically in the case of a CRM strategy.

9.1   Introduction

The implementation of the CRM strategy that has been developed is the next logical step in the CRM process. After the goals and objectives for the CRM strategy have been developed, it is necessary to devise the process for implementing this strategy. Without implementation, the objectives will be no more than words on paper – without any reality. The changes required to enable implementation to take place form the focus of this chapter.

9.2   Prerequisites for the Implementation Strategy

A number of prerequisites exist that an organisation needs to have in place before attempting to implement a CRM strategy. Without these prerequisites, implementation is made more difficult.

- **A shared vision:** It is not enough to have a corporate vision; it is necessary to share the vision with those that will be required to implement the vision. This vision cannot be imposed on the organisation's staff, as this breeds resentment among them. The CEO has to get the co-operation of the staff so as create a sense of ownership and commitment to the vision.[1] This vision is not a document that is kept hidden, but rather something that is an integral part of the way in which the organisation does business. It is knowledge that all the staff members have and need to be reminded of in order for it to affect their behaviour, and for a CRM strategy to be implemented.

- **Decentralisation of authority and management:** This has to do with the place of decision making within the organisation. When authority is decentralised, decisions are made at the lowest level in the organisation, by the people who actually interact with customers. By making these people responsible for decision making, these members of staff are able to show initiative in dealing with customers, so that relationships with customers are improved.

- **The support of top management:** It is the task of the members of top management to direct the activities of the organisation. Without their support in all its forms, the CRM strategy will not be a success. Their support includes the allocation of resources, the development of objectives, the management of reward systems and the development of the organisational structures that support the strategy.[2] Their support is necessary because the implementation of a CRM strategy has far-reaching effects throughout the organisation. Their support can result in overall support at lower levels for the strategy, while also assisting in reducing the degree of resistance to change within the organisation.

It is necessary that top management communicate their intention of implementing the CRM strategy to all levels of staff, thereby giving the strategy the support necessary. This is not to imply that criticism of the strategy is to be suppressed; rather, it indicates that criticism needs to be valid, and, where necessary, it can be incorporated within the strategy as it is adapted over time.

9.3 The Importance of the Implementation Phase in a CRM Strategy

The success of any strategy is determined by whether it attains its objectives or not. This is no different in the case of a CRM strategy. In order to make a success of the CRM strategy, implementation needs to be carefully planned by management.

There are a number of challenges in the implementation of a CRM strategy:[3]

- The scope of any CRM strategy is very broad. This means that it impacts on the entire organisation. This requires changes to be made throughout the organisation, and it is necessary that these changes be well-managed as they are implemented.

- There is a very real possibility that there will be resistance within the organisation to both the implementation of and the need for a CRM strategy. It will require a great deal of leadership and managerial skills for this resistance to be overcome, in order to make the implementation a success.

- The skills that are required to implement a CRM strategy place a great deal of pressure on the managers within the organisation, and where these skills are in short supply, this may cause additional stress and pressure on managers.

One of the techniques that can be used in implementing strategy is the appointment of *sponsors* or *influencers*. These people are specifically selected for their ability to influence the perceptions of others in the organisation, while also being able to lead a team of people coming from divergent departments. They will then be able to appoint others (*change agents*) to assist in the implementation of specific aspects in the various departments (or divisions) within the organisation. This will make it possible to bring about the changes throughout the entire organisation that are required for the successful implementation of any strategy.

9.4 The Development of a Customer Leader

One of the key components to the implementation of any strategy is the person who will provide the inspiration and direction for its implementation. The task of the leader is to take a group of people, mould them into a team and motivate them to achieve a number of objectives.[4] A CRM strategy affects all the parts of the organisation and hence requires this inspiration throughout its functions to facilitate the implementation process.

The characteristics of an effective leader in an organisational context have been widely debated and researched. Effectiveness can be described from a number of different perspectives, such as the skills that leaders have or the behaviour that they exhibit. In the case of CRM, the leader has a slightly different role to play, namely that of making the employees of the organisation customer- and CRM-oriented.

It is suggested that a specific management and leadership concept exists for managing customers and the relationships that are created with customers. This concept seeks to build a technological environment that attempts to integrate the marketing, sales, service and supply-chain functions to enable the staff to provide superior customised and personalised service to customers. It requires specific leadership skills to implement the CRM strategy in the organisation – what can be known as customer relationship leadership (CRL). This customer-oriented leader has the task of aligning the organisation (and its employees) to the goals of the CRM strategy that has been developed for the organisation.[5] This would mean that the customer-oriented leader has to ensure that the goals set for CRM are consistent with the goals of the organisation, while also ensuring that the employees have clarity concerning the goals of the CRM strategy.

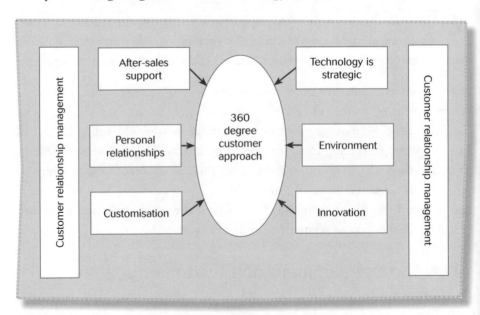

Figure 9.1 The Relationship between CRM and CRL[6]

The selection of a CRM strategy can have major implications for an organisation, so correct implementation of the strategy is required. CRL seeks to integrate the key components of the CRL process so as to maximise the returns from the CRM strategy.

The relationship between CRM and CRL can be seen in figure 9.1. The components of the CRM strategy include customisation, after-sales service and the development of personal relationships with customers. The customers are the core of the model, as they are the reason for the existence of the organisation. The CRL philosophy identifies technology, organisational environment and innovation as the keys to implementation.

In order to implement this concept, changes in a number of key areas are needed, namely in the areas of technology, processes and people.

9.5   Changes in Technology

The recent changes in technology have brought about significant changes in the way in which business and specifically CRM can be done. For a leader in the organisation, it is vital that changes be brought about in technology to make it possible to implement the CRM strategy. The effect of technology is strategic within the organisation, especially in the case of CRM. The technology will enable the organisation to not only stay up to date with its customers, but also to collect additional information with every transaction that takes place. The technologies that have been developed for specific CRM applications are known as information and communications technologies (better known by the abbreviation ICT). These technologies enable the implementation of CRM within the organisation. There are two main aspects to these technologies, namely the front-office applications (which are integrated with the customer database) and the customer contact and access channels.[7]

9.5.1 Implementing New Technology

New technology causes confusion in the minds of staff, and there needs to be a great deal of care regarding the decision as to which software will most adequately satisfy the needs of the CRM strategy. Examples of technology that can be introduced are the Internet, as well as CRM software that is able to track and update the customer database. Examples of these include customer support and service (CSS) software and sales force automation software. New software is continually being developed that can be used to collect and interpret customer data, as well as evaluate the customer behaviour being exhibited. Adoption of the new technology may be a problem, but this change management process has to be managed by the leader. The development of software specific for the organisation can also be considered, depending on its needs.

9.5.2 Training in New Technology

When the new technology has been selected and purchased, it is important to train the staff in using the technology to its full capacity. This means that not only is the initial training vital in making the staff able to use the technology, but it is also necessary to continue with the training as more advanced applications are introduced. Training courses can be customised to meet the specific needs that the staff are experiencing.

The challenge that technology presents is that it is real-time technology, and as such is required to support decision making. These decisions are made continually and not once-off, as they may have been done in the past.[8] This also places pressure on the technology to be reliable and stable. This means that the information that it provides should be consistent and that the system should not 'crash' on a regular basis.

9.5.3 Integration of Technology within the Organisation

In large organisations with many divisions, it has been known that the technology used by the various divisions is not complementary. This means that the systems used in one department are not accessible to other departments. It also means that the customers are inconvenienced, as there are no standard forms available for their use and they are required to submit new applications with all their details, rather than just to alter the existing information.

The example illustrates not only the importance of technology within CRM, but also that the leader is required to integrate these various systems to the benefit of the customer.

> In the case of a financial institution, one division, such as home loans, may use a different form of technology from the credit card division. This means that if a person wants to increase his/her credit limit, he/she is required to submit proof of identity, income, etc. that another division of the bank already has in its possession. This creates the impression that the bank is highly inefficient, and it is frustrating for the customer.[9]

9.6   Changes in Processes

Processes refer to *the way in which things are done to enable the strategy to be implemented successfully*, and CRM requires that the processes be arranged around the customer.[10] Processes need to be developed around the customer and his/her needs, and they can be used to govern the relationship that is created between the organisation and the customer.[11] The processes that are referred to include the expectations and commitments that are part of the relationship, the roles that the various parties play in the relationship and the time that will be committed to the relationship.

Processes refer not only to those things that affect the customer, but also to the way in which relationships are managed within the organisation, which includes the organisational structure and the corporate culture that exists. The organisational processes include the automation of the selling process, which can assist in tracking both the sales and the process of the order.[12] CRM strategy requires changes in the processes within the organisation in a number of different areas.

9.6.1   Implementing Changes in Organisational Processes

Here we refer to the changes that the organisation needs to bring about with respect to internal processes such as administration procedures in order to implement a CRM strategy. These processes need to be integrated with the technology selected by the organisation for the CRM strategy.

> Forms and documentation may not always be compatible with the new technology. The database may require the inclusion of fields that are not part of the documentation, requiring those capturing the data to omit these items. But these items may, at later points, determine key actions that are required within the strategy. This may include customer information that has not been collected. Ideally, data needs to be inputted by the customer directly, which can eliminate errors in processing, as there is no transfer process.

A further organisational process that may change has to do with the institution of a management team to manage the CRM strategy. A CRM strategy team is suggested as a method of governing the relationship between the organisation and its customers in terms of the new CRM strategy being implemented. This team would involve a group of people, including the management of the organisation and key customers.[13] This team has the task of expressing and clarifying the rights of all the parties in relation to the new system, including those of the customer.

This may require the organisation to give up a degree of control over the marketing activities in the organisation, which is not necessarily a popular idea, and may be subject to varying degrees of resistance. It is suggested that the membership of this team be temporary in nature, and that meetings take place on a quarterly basis to facilitate the relationship.

9.6.2 Implementing Changes in Corporate Culture

Corporate culture is a key determinant of the long-term success of CRM strategy implementation. Corporate culture refers to *the common characteristics that exist within the organisation that express the traditions, values, customs and practices that characterises the people who work there.*[14] The culture is largely intangible, yet it reflects the way in which things are done within the organisation. The corporate culture of an organisation can be seen in the shared values, the norms of behaviour that are exhibited, and the symbols and symbolic values that are reflected within the organisation.[15] The purpose of the culture is to bring together a group of diverse people and bind them together so that they can strive towards achieving common goals. The culture of the organisation is determined by the management, specifically the top management.

> A practical example of corporate culture can be seen in the dress code for work. There are organisations where coming to work in shorts and T-shirts is perfectly acceptable. This is a reflection of the corporate culture that exists. There are also many other organisations where this style of dressing would antagonise the management, as it goes counter to the organisations' culture. It is the culture that determines whether a particular style of dressing or type of behaviour is acceptable within a specific context.

Four types of corporate culture can be identified:[16]

- **Power culture:** Usually found in smaller organisations, this kind of culture is defined by a central person, a power source. This person (or group of people) has the power, hence the organisation tends to be political in nature and employees tend to display a tendency to power, politics and risk taking.
- **Person culture:** Here, the individual determines the culture, and the culture of the organisation is subordinate to the individual. Control mechanisms, such as budgets, will only be successful if there is consensus regarding their use.
- **Role culture:** As a bureaucracy, there is great emphasis placed on the role played by each person within the organisation. The power source is the position that the individual holds.

▼ **Job culture:** This is linked to the implementation of a specific project, where the team is required to complete a specific task by co-operating with the other people who are concerned.

The corporate culture can either be an obstacle or a catalyst in the process of strategy implementation. If the culture is supportive, it will make the implementation of the strategy more successful (and much easier), while if the strategy is an obstacle, changes in the culture will be needed if the strategy is to be implemented successfully.[17]

The ideal situation comes about when the strategy and the corporate culture are in agreement, which means that the culture is supportive of the strategy selected. This means that there are no underlying impediments to the implementation process. Should aspects of the CRM strategy be in conflict with the culture, it will be necessary to bring about changes to the culture if the strategy is to be a success. This is a long-term process and one that does not take place easily.

The implementation of a CRM strategy may have an impact on the culture of the organisation. The CRM strategy is one that has a high customer focus, and this may require changes in employees' behaviour towards customers. It may also require longer working hours, or hours that are more convenient to the customer, while being more inconvenient for the staff.

> Woolworths food stores are open until 9 p.m. at night. This is to enable their customers to shop at hours that are convenient to them. However, this means that the store is open at hours that are inconvenient to staff, which has necessitated a change in shifts, as well as a willingness among staff to provide service at different hours from those that are regarded as the norm.

Cultural change is brought about by top management, and is a long-term process.[18] This change takes place as a result of the changes brought about among staff, as well as through deliberate actions of the top management of the organisation. Leadership, and especially the development of a customer leader, can affect the corporate culture and change it towards that of a customer orientation.[19] Without this change in corporate culture, the necessary support for the strategy may not exist, making its long-term success questionable.

9.6.3 Implementing Training Programmes

In order to implement a high-customer-focus strategy such as a CRM strategy, it is necessary that training be conducted among the staff so as to enable them not only to deal with the situations presented by the customers, but also to use the CRM technology efficiently. Both of these require effective training programmes for all staff. It means that the staff need to be trained at times suited to them and on topics that they feel are important, not necessarily as determined by the organisation and the training department. This may mean the development of smaller courses, or where only parts of the courses are presented to satisfy a specific need. Extensive consultation with staff will be required for this to be implemented.

9.6.4 Developing Organisational Structures that Support the CRM Strategy

It may also be necessary to adapt the structure of the organisation to reflect the change in strategy. The structure that is developed within the organisation is one that needs to support the strategy, and much has been written concerning the strategy–structure relationship, as well as the nature and types of structures that can be used. Care needs to be taken in the selection of an organisational structure, and, under certain circumstances, it may be necessary to make adjustments to the strategy to increase its effectiveness.

Various factors affect the selection of an appropriate organisational structure. These factors can be divided up into three main categories:[20]

- **Internal factors:** These refer to those issues that are found within the organisation that can have an effect on the structure. Examples of these factors include the skills levels of the staff, the motivation and leadership styles, as well as the culture of the organisation.

- **External factors:** These factors refer to the environment of the area/city, region and country in which the organisation operates, as well as the international environment in which it operates.

- **Market factors:** These refer to the competitors that can be identified in the environment, the organisation's customers, the product (or service) complexity and the technological changes that can be identified.

After examining these factors, the organisation will be required to select an appropriate organisational structure. The aim of the structure will be to attain the goals of the organisation, which is the implementation of the CRM strategy. This new strategy will require different levels of responsibility from employees, while also requiring different skills and leadership.

9.7   Changing the Way in which People Work

One of the most important aspects in implementing any strategy is to bring about changes in people and the way in which they do their work. Part of trying to implement change is dealing with people's inherent tendency to resist such change. This resistance to change comes about from the fear of the unknown, as well as the uncertainty that accompanies any change. It is seen in people's reluctance to implement new methods, systems and ways of working, or in their tendency to make more errors.

Reasons for resistance to change are diverse.[21] Various reasons include:

- **Inertia:** This implies that staff are content with the current way in which things are done, and they are reluctant to do things differently.

- **Time pressures:** If people are under time pressure, there resistance to change increases, as they are required to put more effort into getting the job done in a shorter time.

- **Surprise:** If the changes are unexpected and there has been little psychological preparation for them, resistance is more likely.

- **Peer pressure:** Where a group is cohesive, its members will stand together regarding their opinion of the change, and this can increase the degree of resistance to change.

- **Self-interest:** Resistance to change comes about when it is not clear how the person will be affected by the change being proposed. Resistance reflects insecurity regarding people's future with respect to changes that are taking place.

- **Uncertainty:** This creates a situation where employees are not sure about their position or how change will affect them. Too little information and communication will increase the levels of uncertainty regarding the various aspects of the changes that are being considered.

It will be necessary for the leader to counter resistance to change if the implementation of the strategy is to be successful. Strategies that can be used to counter resistance to change include education of the staff regarding the proposed changes in strategy, communication regarding the nature of the changes, and encouraging the participation and involvement of all staff members in the implementation process itself.

The change process will have to be managed by the organisation's leaders in order to ensure that the desired changes are implemented by employees, and that they have bought into the changes and are prepared to implement them fully.

9.8 The Importance of Communication in the Implementation of CRM

Communication within the organisation is essential in the implementation of the CRM strategy. Without the communication of information to employees, there will be increased resistance to change, lower degrees of participation in the change process and a bad motivational effect on staff.

The relationship with customers is managed through communication with them through a two-way flow of information. This is done through the organisation communicating with each customer in his/her preferred way — whether using the telephone, email or SMS.[22] It is essential that when a customer initiates contact, he/she is channelled to those employees within the organisation most suited to dealing with the issues being raised. The employees who deal with the customer need to record the communication and need to be trained in handling the complaints and comments made by the customer.

9.9 Control of a CRM Strategy

A strategy is not implemented without first making decisions regarding how to determine its success. Any strategy will have key areas that will determine whether it was successful in achieving its goal. The CRM strategy is one that requires a great deal of investment on the part of the organisation, and it is necessary to determine if it has been successful. The success of any strategy is determined by the objectives that have been set for the strategy.

Indicators of the strategy's success include:[23]

- revenue increases that occur as a result of the strategy, as well as the associated decline in costs;
- the acquisition of new customers;
- good retention rates of existing customers;
- high revenues and profitability for new customers in comparison to existing customers;
- acquiring competitors' share of business; and
- acquiring competitors' share of core customers' business.

9.10 Summary

In order to implement a CRM strategy, it is necessary to have the right technology, the right processes and the right people. The implementation process depends on first having these three key components in place, and then fully implementing the CRM strategy. These three components need to be adapted where necessary to ensure the success of the CRM strategy. It is also necessary to pay attention to the way in which control will take place in order to determine whether the strategy has been successfully implemented.

Discussion Questions

1. Why is implementation important in a CRM strategy?
2. Why is leadership important in a CRM strategy?
3. What is meant by CRL?
4. What are the components of CRL?
5. In what three key areas are changes needed if the implementation of a CRM strategy is to be successful?
6. How can technology affect the implementation of a CRM strategy?
7. How do changes in processes affect the implementation of a CRM strategy?
8. How can leaders overcome resistance to change?
9. Why is communication important in the implementation of a CRM strategy?
10. How can the implementation of a CRM strategy be controlled?

Mini Case Study

Steve's Stationers

(Note: This company is fictitious.)

Steven de Waal operates a stationery company in Johannesburg. He started the business in 1978, opening a store in the downtown CBD. His primary market was the businesses in the CBD, but there was also a significant percentage of sales to passing trade. Over time, Steven opened more branches of the business in shopping malls in various parts of Johannesburg. Each of the stores had significant corporate support in its specific area. There are currently 11 stores around Johannesburg, and Steven has planned to open new stores in other centres around South Africa. An investigation into Steven's business has indicated that the corporate sector makes up 70 per cent of the business conducted. These corporate clients spend an average of R900 per month on stationery supplies.

The stationery market is very competitive. Not only are there many small stationery stores, but stationery is also sold in supermarkets, while there has been a concerted effort on the part of some wholesalers to sell more stationery, using price discounting specifically to do so. It is in this competitive market that Steven trades.

An examination of Steven's corporate clients indicates that 20 per cent of clients contribute 80 per cent of the profits of the organisation. The remaining 80 per cent of clients cause the greatest amount of administration work for the staff in Steven's stationery store. Many of these clients do not pay their accounts on time, and it requires extensive follow-up for the monies owing to be collected.

Steven is the CEO of the business, and there is a geographic structure within the organisation. Each store has a branch manager, and it is each manager's responsibility to contact the functional manager regarding his/her stock and staff requirements. Each store has a computer system, but this is not connected by means of a server or network system. The marketing manager has a number of sales representatives who visit the various businesses in order to gain orders. Each order placed is delivered within 24 hours.

Steven has decided that a CRM strategy is required to improve profits in the corporate market.

Questions

1. Formulate the objectives for Steven's CRM strategy.
2. Explain the technology that Steven will need to use to implement the CRM strategy.
3. Explain the changes in processes that will be required to implement the strategy.
4. Explain the changes in people that will be required to implement the CRM strategy.
5. How will Steven determine whether the strategy has been successful?

References

1   Galbreath, J & Rogers, T. 1999. Customer relationship leadership: A leadership and motivational model for twenty-first century business. *The TQM Magazine*, 11 (3), p. 168.

2   Du Plessis, PJ, Jooste, CJ & Strydom, JW. 2001. *Applied Strategic Marketing*. Sandown: Heinemann, p. 396.
3   Gordon, IH. 1998. *Relationship Marketing*. Toronto: John Wiley, p. 160.
4   Oosthuizen, TFJ (ed.). 2002. *Managerial Tasks for Managerial Success*. Johannesburg: Entropro, p. 79.
5   Galbreath & Rogers, *op. cit.*, p. 165.
6   *Ibid.*, p. 170.
7   Koen, JPL. 2001. *Customer Relationship Management ... the Tool that Will Win and Keep Customers*. Johannesburg: Wits Business School.
8   Gordon, *op. cit.*, p. 66.
9   Galbreath & Rogers, *op. cit.*, p. 161.
10 *Ibid.*, p. 31.
11 *Ibid.*, p. 65.
12 Koen, *op. cit.*, p. 3.
13 Gordon, *op., cit.*, p. 162.
14 Wilson, AM. 2001. Understanding organisational culture and the implications for corporate marketing. *European Journal of Marketing*, 35 (3/4), p. 354.
15 Du Plessis *et al.*, *op. cit.*, p. 395.
16 Smit, PJ & Cronjé, GJ de J. 1992. *Management Principles*. Cape Town: Juta, p. 392.
17 Du Plessis, *op. cit.*, p. 396.
18 Wilson, *op. cit.*, p. 355.
19 *Ibid.*, p. 357.
20 Du Plessis, *op. cit.*, p. 392.
21 Smit & Cronjé, *op. cit.*, p. 252.
22 Koen, *op. cit.*, p. 4.
23 Gordon, *op. cit.*, pp. 163–64.

Index